NEWPORT BASEBALL

HISTORY

NEWP⚾RT

BASEBALL

— HISTORY —

AMERICA'S PASTIME IN THE CITY BY THE SEA

RICK HARRIS

Charleston · London

THE
History
PRESS

Published by The History Press
Charleston, SC 29403
www.historypress.net

First published 2014

Manufactured in the United States

ISBN 978.1.62619.452.6

Library of Congress CIP data applied for.

This book is in memory of my mother, Katie "Home Run" Hudson (Priolo) (1929–1999), a barehanded third base-person who handled the hot corner for her Maxwell, Iowa softball team and lofted a good many balls over the left-field fence. She was also one of the most encouraging and kindest people I have ever known.

CONTENTS

Acknowledgements

Tabitha Dulla, commissioning editor at The History Press

Will Collicott, project editor at The History Press

Len Levin, retired chief copy editor at the *Providence Journal* and baseball historian, editing assistance

Emily Harris, editing assistance

Salve Regina University:
Eric Cirella, head baseball coach
Edward Habershaw, sports information director
Susan Small, circulation supervisor, McKillop Library
Joe Foley, manager, McKillop Library
Julie C. Swierczek, university archives librarian

George Donnelly Jr., baseball historian

St. George's School:
Valerie Simpson, library archivist
Will Simpson, research volunteer, class of 2014
Andrew Lynch, research volunteer, class of 2014

ACKNOWLEDGEMENTS

Chris La Rose, commissioner, George Donnelly Sunset League

Bob Cvornyek, PhD, chair of the History Department at RIC and African American baseball historian

Edward Harrigan, administrator, Newport Recreation Department

Joe Baker, *Newport News* reporter

INTRODUCTION

I have been researching and writing about baseball in America since 1990. Originally, I had the goal of writing a simple but comprehensive book about the history of baseball in Rhode Island. However, I quickly realized that this would not be possible, as my research began to uncover literally thousands of stories about people, places and events. I have read thousands and thousands of firsthand accounts about baseball and the people who played the game. I've interviewed hundreds of ex-players, family members and individuals whose distant relatives played the game in past centuries. I've held in my hands old photos and the actual artifacts used 100 to 150 years past and intrinsically felt the stories contained within. As I explored all this information, I came to realize that the only way to tell the story is not to tell *the story* at all but to write about the many treasured nuggets of small stories hidden in the collective minds of Rhode Islanders and the collective writings of many authors of firsthand accounts.

With this in mind, this book represents "slices of life and baseball" that rose up to the surface through the vast storehouse of information contained in diaries, newspapers, old magazines, ancient books, family stories and, last but not least, the old but vibrant memories of individuals. However, those of you who like chronology and statistics should not despair—there is also plenty of that in this book, as well as in my previous two books about Rhode Island baseball published by The History Press. Collectively, the stories in this book—especially when added to those found in the other two books—paint a very comprehensive story of baseball not just in Newport

Washington Square, Newport, 1895. *Author's collection.*

or even Rhode Island but in all the nooks and crannies of America. I recommend reading the whole set, as well as setting forth on your own exploration of your neighborhood, town, city and/or state to unearth the treasures that lie just beneath the surface, waiting for someone like you to bring them to light.

RICK HARRIS

P.S. In order to write interesting stories about baseball in Rhode Island, one must organize tens of thousands of pieces of information. I have developed large library databases, which I provide freely upon request—just ask.

Chapter 1

WELCOME TO NEWPORT: NEWPORT'S PLACE IN EARLY AMERICAN HISTORY

When you tug on a single thread in nature, you will find it attached to everything else.
—*John Muir*

John Muir's quote applies not only to physical nature but also to the interweaving of human history. Developing a broad understanding of the human activity we call baseball requires a look at the total history of human habitation of a given area—in this case, Newport. Only then can one understand all the threads that make up the community and, ultimately, baseball.

Greetings from Newport, 1909. *Author's collection.*

Why Is Newport History Important in a Book about Newport Baseball?

The answer is this: In order to understand how baseball teams were formulated and stayed in business, one must also understand the nature and constitution of the community. The mix of baseball teams that developed in Newport is extremely different than the variety found in other Rhode Island communities. Below are a few types of baseball teams:

- Teams in youth programs such as Little League and Babe Ruth
- Private/public elementary school, junior high school and high school teams
- College/university teams
- Fraternal sponsorship (i.e., Knights of Columbus) teams
- Adult amateur teams
- Mill/Industrial/Business-Sponsored
- Military teams
- Town teams
- Semiprofessional teams
- Professional teams

Not included in the above list are myriad travel-type teams, among them the House of David, major- and minor-league barnstorming teams, traveling black baseball teams, Bloomer Girls teams and novelty concerns such as donkey baseball.

In the late 1800s and early 1900s, there were more than 450 "localities" in Rhode Island, each hosting a mix of adult baseball teams. In some communities, the localities were actually numerous villages, of which only a few are known today. In Burrillville, located in the northwest corner of Rhode Island, these included Bridgeton, Gazzaville, Glendale, Graniteville, Harrisville, Laurel Hill, Mapleville, Nasonville, Oak Valley, Oakland, Pascoag, Tarkiln, Saxonville, Wallum Lake and Whipple. Newport, on the other hand, was different, as these localities consisted not of villages but rather self-identified neighborhoods or geographic locations. Some of these areas are likely known now only by older residents or enthusiastic students of history, and fewer still would know the origin of the names. Newport's localities include Bishop Rock, Brenton Point, Brenton Village, Castle Hill, Cherry Neck, Coasters Harbor Island, Coddington Point, Goat Island, Goose Neck, Gooseberry Island, Graves Point, Lands End, Lime Rock,

Point of Trees, Rose Island, Rough Point and Sheep Point. Unlike most communities in Rhode Island, Newport localities are based primarily on geographic formations such as "points" and islands.

All communities in Rhode Island sponsored public school–based youth teams. With the exception of Newport, almost every city and town had approximately the same ratio regarding the type and mix of adult baseball teams, largely determined by the size of the municipality. For example, Woonsocket in 1920 hosted twelve industrial amateur/semipro teams. There were no teams in Woonsocket that existed independent of a mill, factory or business concern. Newport, however, contrasts almost all other Rhode Island communities. In 1920, for instance, Newport hosted two independent semipro teams and several military teams, as well as the beginning of independent organized amateur ball in the newly formed Sunset League (1919). There were no strictly mill/industrial teams. The answer to why Newport is different can be found in its history.

(Please excuse the following small excursions into non-baseball historical avenues. To someone who likes to write about history, a good story is a story that has to be told. If John Muir is correct—and I believes he is—this is justified because all things are connected and contribute to the character of the community.)

WHO WAS FIRST?

From the beginning of human habitation in the Newport area, the draw has been the surrounding waters. According to several archaeological sources, Rhode Island, including Newport, was first inhabited between 8,000 and 3,000 BCE. Physical remnants of the early inhabitants of Rhode Island are rare because these people were primarily hunters and gatherers with part-time settlements, and not much was left behind. The first permanent settlement discovered in Rhode Island was found on Block Island about 2,500 years ago.

There is considerable controversy regarding the identity of the first non–Native American visitors to the Rhode Island area. Some amateur historians have claimed that the Phoenicians, Carthaginians or Egyptians visited the area during the BCE period. Others have claimed that Rhode Island was first visited by the Vikings. These claims, of course, are all highly

Old Stone Mill, 1908. *Author's collection.*

speculative. One popular tourist destination related to speculation is the Old Stone Tower (also known as the Old Mill) in Newport. Amateur sleuths and treasure hunters alike have made the claim that the tower was built by the Phoenicians, Vikings or possibly the Knights Templar. However, Rhode Island's historian laureate, Dr. Patrick T. Conley, has concluded after extensive research that it was a colonial-era mill. Yet another theory is that the structure was built as a mill by Benedict Arnold, great-grandfather of the Revolutionary War traitor of the same name, who had moved from Providence to Newport in 1653. (The 1600s Benedict Arnold was the first governor of Rhode Island.) Whatever the true story, the structure is symbolic of the many historic sites that have drawn people from all over the world to visit Newport.

Some historians believe that the first European explorer to visit the area was Portugal's Miguel Corte-Real, who was believed to have been shipwrecked in Newport around 1502. It's been speculated that he lived several years with a local tribe of Wampanoag Indians. Some historians suggest that a large sandstone boulder at Assonet Neck and the Taunton River is inscribed with

Corte-Real's name, his family's coat of arms and the year 1511. The late Dr. Manuel Luciano da Silva of Bristol, in his many writings on the subject of Portuguese in America, made a compelling argument for the inscription that has never been scientifically verified. The first confirmed European visitor to the Newport area was the explorer Giovanni da Verrazano, who arrived in the area in 1524. The Jamestown-Verrazano Bridge, which helps connect the island chain to the mainland of Rhode Island, is named in his honor.

RELIGIOUS AND ETHNIC DIVERSITY

From the beginning, the Portsmouth-Newport area was a haven for religious diversity and freethinkers. In 1639, under the leadership of Dr. John Clarke, William Coddington and others, with the help of Roger Williams, purchased Aquidneck Island from the local Native Americans. The sons of Nicholas Easton, one of the founders, settled on an island in Newport Harbor and named it Coasters Island. (Coasters Island has been used extensively by the U.S. Navy and has been home to several baseball fields and U.S. Navy baseball teams.) Other members of the founding group considered other locations in Newport, among them the area that is now Thames Street. (That area was too swampy but was later filled in, and a beautiful ballpark was built. The park, which was first called the "Basin," is now nationally known as Cardines Field.) The founding group originally settled in the Newport Beach area, but for fear that it would not be safe for shipping, it moved to an area that is now at the corner of West Broadway and Marlborough Streets. It appears to have been a good choice because of the protected harbor area, and Newport would become a world-class port of commerce.

In addition to being a physician, Dr. John Clarke was also a Baptist minister and was responsible for establishing the second Baptist church in America. (The first was in Providence.) Also prominent in the group of founding members were Quakers, among them Anne Hutchinson. In the definition of the time period, Hutchinson was a strong feminist. She believed in the virtues of the Quaker religion and felt that women had a right to not only be given religious education but also to preach. It was her belief in the Quaker religion that got her and several others banned from Boston, where the Quaker religion was outlawed. A much lesser known story is that of Mary Dyer.

Mary Dyer was the wife of William Dyer, one of the founding members of the community. Like her good friend Hutchinson, Dyer taught and preached the Quaker religion. She was a courageous spokeswoman for her religion. After living in Rhode Island for a period, she returned to England to study religion before coming back to the colonies. Upon stepping off the ship in Boston, she was arrested for being a Quaker and put in jail, where she was confined for three months until her influential spouse, William Dyer, was able to get her release with the promise that she would not return. However, when Mary heard that two fellow Quakers, William Robinson and Marmaduke Stephenson, had been arrested in Boston and sentenced to hang, she traveled to the city to speak on their behalf. Being a Quaker was a capital offense in Boston at the time, and Mary Dyer was sentenced to hang along with the two men. Against her wishes, her son traveled to Boston and successfully intervened. According to historian John Williams Haley, Dyer was on the gallows, but the crowd's strong disapproval of a woman being hanged saved her life. Because of her strong convictions, she returned for a third time to Boston in 1660 to preach. She was subsequently arrested and hanged on June 1. Her crime was her religion.

Jews also came to Newport to escape religious persecution. Many Jewish families settled in the Newport area beginning in the mid-1600s, with the first families coming from Holland. Later, in the seventeenth and early eighteenth centuries, Jewish families from Curaçao, Portugal and Spain settled in Newport. The last group of people to immigrate to Newport did so to avoid the Spanish Inquisition. America's oldest existing synagogue, now known as the Touro Synagogue, was begun in 1759 and dedicated in 1763. Many others with diverse religious faiths, including Presbyterians and Catholics, migrated to Newport, creating an extremely ethnically diverse population.

Newport: A Pirate Haven

For much of the late 1600s and early 1700s, Newport was a haven for pirates. Although most of the shipping business was legitimate in nature due to excellent port facilities, the locals' tolerance of less-than-legal activities and Rhode Island's independent nature made Newport a perfect stopover for pirates. The most famous local pirate was Thomas Tew, known as the Rhode Island Pirate, who used Newport as his home base. Although he went on only two major pirating voyages, he became famous for creating what became known as the Pirate Round—a route that included the Caribbean Sea and the Atlantic Ocean. Tew met a violent death in a ship-to-ship gun battle when he was disemboweled by a cannonball. Newport was frequented by many other pirates as well, including William Kidd, Blackbeard and Henry Every. In fact, pirates in Newport became so common that the colony of Rhode Island earned the epithet of "Rogues Island." As the eighteenth century wore on, laws were passed in England and in Rhode Island that made piracy a much more dangerous game. Penalties were stiff. In 1720, twenty-six pirates were hanged just outside Newport and buried on Goat Island. This action had a considerably chilling effect on Newport-based piracy.

THE SLAVE TRADE

In the first half of the 1700s, much of the wealth in Providence, Bristol and Newport came from the shipping trade. A large portion of that was transporting slaves from Africa to the New England area and Newport in particular. According to the National Park Service's Ethnography Program, about one thousand slave-trading voyages left Rhode Island, and most of them traveled from Newport to Africa's Ivory Coast. Ships left Newport carrying rum from Rhode Island's thirty distilleries (twenty-two of which were in Newport) to sail to Africa and bring back slaves. Despite the lucrative trade, Rhode Island outlawed slavery in 1784. Additionally, in 1787, the state prohibited residents from trading in slaves. It should be noted that American Indians were also enslaved during this era. Unfortunately, the fate of the slaves did not improve much after death, as most were buried in the Common Burying Ground on Newport's Farewell Street.

One interesting anecdote, as noted in Louis Cappelli's *Rhode Island: A Guide to the Smallest State* (1937) is that in 1756, a group of Newport slaves got together to hold a mock election. Slaves who owned a "pig and sty" were allowed to vote, mimicking Rhode Island's law requiring land ownership to vote. A "governor" and other officials were elected, and the inauguration was held on the corner of Thames and Farewell Streets. According to the report, the newly elected governor, elected officials, losing candidates and others joined in a jubilant celebration filled with dancing and "spirits."

Newport Winter Carnival with winter baseball, circa 1910. *Author's collection.*

BEGINNING IN THE TOURIST TRADE

Newport has long been known as a tourist destination and, for the wealthy, as a place of "summering." The tourist trade actually began in the mid-1700s. Unlike most Rhode Island communities, whose economies centered on manufacturing and the production of woolen goods, Newport relied on commerce for its economic base. Wealthy Newport families put on numerous festivals to attract visitors. This tradition continued well into the 1900s, as evidenced by the photo of a winter folk festival complete with a baseball game. More on the tourist industry, which, along with the military, had a great impact on the types of baseball teams Newport hosted.

Prewar Activities

Perhaps a bit of the old "Rogues Island" sentiment remained well into the mid-1700s. Newport was the scene of several actions of civil disobedience against the Crown, some of which turned violent. Today, in public schools across America, children are taught about the Boston Tea Party, a rebellious act in 1773 in response to the tea tax imposed by Parliament. Rhode Islanders are also familiar with the burning of the *Gaspee* in 1772 off Gaspee Point in Warwick. However, these actions were predated by several that occurred in Newport.

In 1764, Newporters responded violently to the seizure from Howland's Ferry of cargo and sugar being transported by the British schooner *St. John's*. When the British man-of-war *Squirrel* attempted to intervene, an angry mob went to a battery nearby and started shelling both vessels. The man-of-war then opened fire, dispersing the mob. A year later, another incident occurred. It was common practice for British warships to "press" sailors from private ships into the Crown's service—sort of an "in the wrong place at the wrong time" military draft mechanism. In May 1765, the British ship *Maidstone* pressed a number of sailors to serve in the British Navy and later pressed the whole crew of a ship from Africa. Once again, a mob gathered. It seized one of the *Maidstone*'s boats, dragged it to the Common and burned it. In July 1769, the British ship *Liberty* brought a captured Connecticut brig and sloop into harbor. During the night, a group of Newporters cut the lines of the *Liberty* and burned the ship when it drifted to shore near Long Wharf. These were all blatant acts of rebellion against the British government several years before the colonists would begin their long journey to independence through war.

The Beginning of the "Basin" (Cardines Field)

An entire section in this book is dedicated to Cardines Field, originally known simply as the "Basin." During the colonial period, much of what is now America's Cup Avenue, Brick Market Place and the Tourist Center was swamp. In the 1770s, indentured servants and Native American and African American slaves were forced to fill in parts of the swamp to create a waterfront. This was the very beginning of what later would become the ball field known at different times as the Railroad Grounds, the Basin and, finally, Cardines Field. With these "public works" modifications, one of the

The Basin, circa 1870. *Courtesy George Donnelly Jr.*

best-protected harbors on the East Coast was developed. By 1790, Newport's population had grown to 6,717, making it the eighth-largest city in the new United States, just ahead of Providence. The strategic importance of the city of Newport was not lost on the British. Whoops, we are getting ahead of ourselves.

WAR AND OCCUPATION COME TO NEWPORT

On December 7, 1776, a British fleet under the command of Sir Peter Parker sailed up the Sakkonet River and landed with nine thousand English and Hessian troops in Middletown. The following day, British general Sir Henry Clinton took possession of Newport; the British would remain in control for the next three years. Times during the occupation were harsh for the Newport residents, who had been forced to give up their homes, material goods and food to the occupying force. In July 1778, a French fleet under the command of Count D'Estaing entered Newport Harbor, and the British ships moved out to sea. The French moved out after them, and a terrible storm caused the dispersion of both fleets. The French ships briefly stopped in Newport Harbor but moved on to Boston, leaving the British still in occupation of Newport. The departure of the French ships resulted in the retreat of General John Sullivan of New Hampshire, who had been prepared to attack Newport to drive out the British. During the retreat, Rhode Island's only major Revolutionary War land conflict occurred—a fight that became known as the Battle of Rhode Island. Neither side could declare victory.

In October 1779, the British masters of Newport were ordered back to New York, and by October 26, American troops had reoccupied the city. The next occupation by a foreign power was a friendly one—a French contingent under the leadership of General Rochambeau, hero to America. This occupation had a stabilizing effect from the perspective of the American colonists. A review of the *Newport Mercury* indicates that things returned to a semblance of normalcy for the next couple years, at least as much as could be expected during a major war. Great tensions still existed between remaining Loyalists (Tories) and Revolutionaries, resulting in the land of Tories and sympathizers being confiscated and redistributed. On March 6, 1781, General George Washington came to Newport to visit General Rochambeau. To demonstrate the unity between France and America, King Louis XVI authorized General Washington to wear "Le Marshall de la France uniforme," symbolizing Washington's command over the French troops and navy in America.

In 1783, America gained its independence. In terms of lives lost, the war was costly on both sides. Since detailed records were not kept, all casualty figures are estimates. The United States lost 25,000 soldiers—8,000 in battle and 17,000 due to disease, starvation and accidents. Although British and Hessian casualties were somewhat higher at 27,297, fewer died in battle (2,440), with the remaining 24,857 deaths the result of disease and accidents. In my opinion, higher casualties for the colonists were most likely caused by inexperience (both in leadership and soldiering), a lack of technologically advanced weaponry and weakness caused by illness and lack of nutrition.

Postwar Development

In the eighteenth century and through the beginning of the nineteenth century, Newport was a favored seaport for European trade. As other seaports (including Providence) developed up and down the Atlantic, Newport began to lose its grip on commerce. Economic development was at a standstill. Unlike what was happening in other communities in Rhode Island, Newport's manufacturing remained undeveloped with only a few endeavors. The lack of industrial development is a critical factor that would eventually determine the types of baseball teams to play in Newport.

The Beginning of the Tourism Industry

In about 1830, Newport became a summer destination for wealthy southerners and patrons from Cuba. One thing Newport lacked was hotel accommodations, which, for some unknown reason, were not developed. However, the lagging hotel industry resulted in a residential boom as visitors simply started buying and developing land, first as summer cottages and later as mansions. This investment in the community by the wealthy summer residents (along with the heavy military presence in Newport) had a tremendous impact on the composition of the baseball teams that became part of the community by the end of the century. By the mid-1850s, tourism was alive and well, and Newport was poised for an economic growth spurt to last well into the 1880s. This transformation is described in detail by Frank G. Harris in *History of the Re-Union of the Sons and Daughters of the Revolution* (1884):

> *In looking over the years that have passed since the reunion of 1859, one sees many changes—changes that indicate great prosperity and marked a steady uniform growth of the City. Commerce we have little or none, and our manufacturers have nearly or quite died out, though we have not come to a stand. The energies of the people have been turned into new channels, and the many find employment provided for the hundreds of thousands who annually flock to this seaside. In 1859 the taxable property of Newport was valued at $10,484,400; today it is set at $27,543,600, and the savings banks are oppressed by the amount of their deposits. Sections of the City that were then only field land are now laid out and built over—not wholly for summer residences, but with the homes a great part for a well-to-*

*do population; as witness the upper part of Broadway and the streets that
radiate from the great thoroughfare.*

*The efforts to make Newport a manufacturing place have signally failed.
Twenty-five years ago many mill hands here found employment, but in
1860 the Coddington factory, which turned out 50,000 yards of print
copper per week, was destroyed by fire. Then came the destruction of the
woolen mill by the same element, which had often injured it before. The
Aquidneck Mill was partially destroyed by fire but was restored again and
put in working order. For a time it was run after that, but eventually the
machinery was taken out, and there it stands, still unoccupied. The Point
factory was burnt, the lead works and shot tower have long been idle, and
the Perry Mill, built in 1835, is the only one running. The fine building
put up on Marlborough Street for the Newport Manufacturing Company
is now owned by the Newport Water Works. But business of other kinds
has so improved as to make it almost imperative that at no distant day
Thames Street must either be widened or a new street, along the waterfront,
be provided to accommodate the traffic.*

*During the war [the Civil War] Goat Island and Fort Wolcott were
used by the Navy Department for the Naval Academy, in connection with
the Atlantic House. When peace was declared and there was talk of sending
the Academy back to Annapolis, the City offered to give Coasters Harbor
Island to the Government if it would plant the Academy there; an offer that
was declined, for it was thought best that it should occupy its old quarters*

The famous First Beach in Newport, circa 1899. *Author's collection.*

26

Roller coaster and boardwalk on Newport Beach, 1908. *Author's collection.*

in Maryland. A few years later the Navy established a school on Goat Island, for instruction and torpedo practice. To this end work shops, store houses, and laboratories were provided, and the Island has been dotted with cottages for the use of instructors. The officer in charge has his quarters in what was the old barracks of Fort Wolcott, which are made a commodious and pleasant residence.

The chapter goes on to describe many public works improvements (including ocean breaches) and the coming of the railroad and steamship industries, which, of course, brought more tourism. The advent of the military presence and its expansion had a significant impact on the development of baseball in Newport, a topic that will be covered later.

IDAWALLEY (IDA) ZORADA LEWIS

I would be remiss not to mention a very important historical Newport figure in one Ida Lewis. As an old saying goes, "God broke the mold when he made Ida Lewis."

IDA LEWIS AGAIN HONORED
To Be Recipient of Pension for Remainder of Her Life
Awarded $30 a Month by Andrew Carnegie from His Private Pension Fund

Ida Lewis Wilson has received many honors for her heroism in saving lives in Newport Harbor. On July 4th, 1860, she was presented by the city of Newport with a handsome rowboat fitted with a silver rudder yoke by the Narragansett Yacht Club of Providence and a set of Colors from the officers of Steamer city of Newport. Later the late James Fisk renamed a boathouse on Lime Rock for housing the boat. During the years since that time she has been presented with many medals by the United States government and by societies.
—Newport News, *November 21, 1907*

Ida Lewis is one of Newport's most famous women. She was the daughter of Captain Hosea Lewis, the keeper of Lime Rock Lighthouse in Newport in 1854. Hosea Lewis had been at Lime Rock Lighthouse less than four months when he suffered a stroke. Ida took over the chores of the lighthouse, becoming very skillful at rowing between the island and the city of Newport to take her three siblings to school each day, even in the winter. She also became known as Newport's best swimmer.

Ida's first rescue came in the fall of 1858, when she was only seventeen years old. Four young local men were seen rowing between Fort Adams and Lime Rock. One of the young men climbed the mast and began deliberately rocking the boat back and forth, and soon the boat capsized. The young men struggled desperately to cling to the boat. Ida rowed out and rescued all four. She received no recognition for her efforts at that time. Her first famous rescue came on March 29, 1869, when two soldiers passed through Newport Harbor toward Fort Adams in a small boat. Sergeant James Adams and Private John McLaughlin had enlisted the help of a fourteen-year-old boy who told them he knew how to navigate the harbor. A snowstorm turned up the harbor waters, and the boat overturned. With the assistance of her younger brother, Ida saved the soldiers and the boy. The soldiers at Fort Adams collected and gave her $218 for her efforts, and one of the soldiers gave her a gold watch. Ida also became the first woman to receive the Congressional Lifesaving Medal.

Over the next thirty-nine years, Ida Lewis was credited with saving eighteen lives, becoming quite famous for doing so. *Harpers Weekly* and other publications referred to her as the "Bravest Woman in America." Throughout her career, she remained alone on Lime Rock, and she received

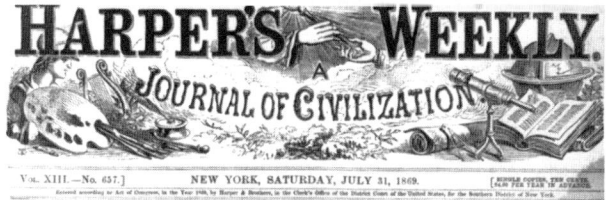

Ida Lewis on the cover of *Harper's Weekly*, July 31, 1869. *Courtesy Library of Congress LC-USZ62-75201.*

many accolades, gifts of money and silver awards. In 1924, the Rhode Island General Assembly renamed Lime Rock the Ida Lewis Rock. In 1995, the U.S. Coast Guard named a buoy tender after her, the cutter *Ida Lewis*, which is stationed in Newport, Rhode Island.

Ida Lewis became ill while tending the lighthouse in 1911 and died on October 25, 1911, at the of age sixty-nine. She left behind the legacy of being one of America's most prominent feminists, although it's doubtful she ever thought of herself in that fashion. A perusal of many contemporary documents relating to Ida Lewis makes it seem likely that she would describe her heroic efforts as simply doing her job.

THE NEWPORT MANSIONS

Newport has many points of interest, perhaps none better known than its mansions. These grand residences have come to symbolize America's Gilded Age, a period of remarkable economic growth beginning in the 1870s and lasting through the early 1900s. Some of America's wealthiest families, including the Vanderbilts and Astors, built extravagant "summer cottages" on Bellevue Avenue and Ocean Drive. Many of these mansions are now open for tours. The influence of these families led to the arrival

Mercury Pub. Co., Newport, R. I. 233

of other attractions, including the America's Cup races, the Newport Tennis Hall of Fame and, early in the twentieth century, the Polo Grounds. These and other developments contributed significantly to the development of the service industry in Newport, which in turn, along with extensive tourism, created the audiences for amateur, semipro and professional baseball teams. These factors also influenced city government in developing recreational facilities, including parks, attractions such as the Cliff Walk and, of course, ball fields.

Vanderbilt Mansion, 1905.
Author's collection.

THAMES STREET.

The famous Ocean Drive Cliff Walk, 1909. *Author's collection.*

Opposite, top: Bellevue Avenue, 1905. *Author's collection.*

Opposite, bottom: Thames Street, 1884. *Author's collection.*

LEAVING NEWPORT—COME BACK SOON

We have now identified the most significant aspects of the City by the Sea's history relevant to the development of baseball: commerce, wealth, the military and people. It is now time to continue our journey and look at the origins and development of baseball in America, Rhode Island and Newport.

Chapter 2

THE ORIGINS AND DEVELOPMENT OF BASEBALL IN AMERICA, RHODE ISLAND AND NEWPORT

AN INTRODUCTION TO THE HISTORY OF THE GRAND OLD GAME THROUGH NEWPORT'S FIRST PUBLISHED BOX SCORE

BASE BALL.—The base ball match between the first nine of the Excelsiors and the second nine of the Seasides, came off in favor of the latter. The following is the score :

EXCELSIORS.	O.	R.	SEASIDE.	O.	R.
W'nship, 2b,	3	2	Robinson, C.,	2	10
Durant, 1b,	1	4	Sands, 3b,	6	4
Wells, R. F.,	4	2	Stedman, 1b,	0	9
Burdick, P.,	1	4	Brewerton, L. F.,	4	5
Robinson, C. F.	7	1	Deblois, 2b,	1	5
Hovey, C.,	3	2	Weed, S. S.,	5	4
McAlister, 3b,	4	3	Barker, P.,	5	4
Vyce, S. S.,	1	5	Norman, C F.,	2	5
Betton, L. F.,	3	2	Peckham, R. F.,	2	7
Total,	27	25		27	53

INNINGS.

	1st,	2d,	3d,	4th,	5th,	6th,	7th,	8th,	9th.	
Excelsior,	3.	3.	4.	7.	2.	0.	2.	1.	3.	25.
Seaside,	2.	5.	1.	8.	9.	6.	13.	4.	5.	53.

Box score from the Excelsiors versus Seasides game. *Newport Daily News*, June 26, 1869. *Author's collection.*

The box score, generally considered the brainchild of New York sportswriter Henry Chadwick, is absolutely the most informative and valuable baseball communication tool ever invented. From the box score, one can understand a considerable amount of the game's story, as well as learn something about the community. In essence, the box score above, although primitive, is a microcosm of the game action, as well as a snapshot of baseball history. Newport's first printed box score tells us the names of the team, which team won, how many runs were scored, player names and positions and how many innings were played. To the baseball historian, the box score tells a lot more than that and is actually reflective of the history of the game. The play-by-play analysis of each inning paints a picture of the hopes and aspirations of the teams' players as the game progresses. For example, by the fourth inning, the Excelsiors were leading the game 17–16, and both teams thought that they had a good shot at winning. However, after the next three innings, we can assume that the excitement of the Seasides players and fans contrasted the total devastation felt by the Excelsiors. In those three innings, the Seasides scored 28 runs to a paltry 4 by their opposition. The game, for all intents and purposes, was almost certainly over, and everyone knew it—well, almost everyone. As per human nature, a small portion of fans and players blessed with a constitution of eternal optimism believed the advantage could still be retaken by the Excelsiors. Hence, the game continued, the losing team's players continued to play hard and the fans continued to watch. In the next century, the famous philosopher Yogi Berra would epitomize this wonderful quirk of human nature by pronouncing, "It ain't over 'til it's over."

Even if we did not know the exact year in which the game was played, closer scrutiny of the box score allows us to provide a fair estimate of the time period. Scores are the first clue. During this phase of baseball, the game was played barehanded. Even though the ball was softer than the one used now, it was still plenty hard, resulting in many errors and, in turn, high-scoring games. The high scoring of both teams would also indicate that the rule that allowed the batter to instruct the pitcher where he wanted the ball thrown may have still been in place. We also note that errors aren't even listed, another clue. Take a look at the offensive categories, of which there were only two. "O" equals the number of times the batter was put out, and "R" represents the number of runs he scored. The names of the teams also indicate an approximate age. In regard to the Excelsiors, the contemporary common meaning of this word—used often by newspapers, hotels and other business—meant "of superior quality," and it was an extremely common baseball team name in the 1860s and 1870s. The name Seasides was used in the late 1860s and early 1870s in conjunction with the Atlantic Seaboard resort communities, giving us a geographic clue as well. In addition, the fact that both team names were pluralized also indicates that the teams were from the late nineteenth century because earlier teams usually had a singular name (e.g., Atlantic, Athletic, etc.).

The baseball historian also needs to be well versed in many disciplines aside from history—including genealogy, sociology, topography and statistical analysis—and should be well read in general human history. For example, by comparing the last names of players in the box scores to genealogy records and census information, we can get a good idea of the popularity or, in some cases, the tolerance of various ethnic groups. Ethnic groups tended to self-segregate themselves or were forced by sociological factors into neighborhoods, localities, towns and even small cities. In the case of the 1869 Newport box score, we may not be able to glean the ethnicity of the general population of Newport, but we can draw some conclusions about the homogeneity of the two teams just by looking at the surnames. If we couple this with genealogical mapping of the area and census data, we can determine whether the team was composed of mostly local individuals or people from elsewhere.

With modern box scores, batting averages, earned-run averages and a host of other statistical information can be determined. The most interesting aspect of baseball is its history, both in statistical and human terms. So thank you, Henry Chadwick, for inventing such a useful tool that efficiently records statistical information with some human historical information elements thrown in. The human story of baseball has come to us passed down through oral tradition and in contemporary writing. Using all sources, we can write about this wonderful human activity we call baseball and learn much about our collective past.

BASEBALL: WHERE AND HOW DID IT ALL BEGIN

Baseball just didn't pop into the heads of humans overnight. The modern game certainly owes gratitude to Alexander Cartwright, who codified an initial set of rules in 1845, and to all those baseball conventions and rule-making committees that took place and continue to take place to this day. There are certainly some people who would place the year 1845 as the beginning of baseball. However, it is my opinion that baseball developed like a folksong—over a number of years—long before the actual rules were set down. As far back as recorded history goes, every single society has played games with a ball and, many times, a stick. Have you ever observed a young child on a walk in the woods pick up a rock and a stick and then try to hit it? Certainly the child is not thinking about baseball but just doing what comes naturally—taking advantage of what nature has provided. It is not beyond reason to assume that our early ancestors did the same. Let us meander back to the first two written mentions of the word "base ball" (baseball) to prove our point. The following comes from a woodcut found in *A Pretty Little Pocket Book*, published in England in 1774:

Base-Ball

The Ball was struck off,
Away flies the Boy
To the next destin'd Post,
And them Home with Joy.

The woodcut displays three young people dressed in seventeenth-century clothing standing around three large ground stakes in an open field (almost like landmark posts), with one child holding a ball. There is no bat visible; however, the three stakes share a remarkably similarity to the "Massachusetts Game" of the 1850s, which used four four-foot stakes.

There are verbal references to baseball being played in 1777 by Continental army soldiers at Valley Forge. The first written account of a baseball game played in America comes from an ordinance passed in Pittsfield, Massachusetts, in 1791 prohibiting the playing of baseball within eighty yards of the Town Meeting House due to broken windows. This would certainly indicate use of a bat and a ball. Another early reference to baseball appears in a New York City newspaper in 1823.

In 1825, the following account was printed in upstate New York's *Daily Gazette*:

A CHALLENGE

The undersigned, all residents of new town of Hampton, with the exception of Asa C. Holland, who has recently removed into Delhi, challenge an equal number of persons in any town in the county of Delaware to meet them at any time at the house of Edward B. Chance, in said town, to play the game of BASE-BALL for the sum of one dollar per game. If a town can be found that will produce the required number, they will have no obligation to play against any selection that can be made from the several towns in the county. Eli Bagley, Edward B. Chase, Henry P. Chance, Ira Peak, Walter C. Peak, H.B. Goodrich, R.F. Thurber, Asa C. Holland & M.L. Bostwick.

Rhode Island has its entry in the early written accounts of baseball in the form of a diary kept in 1827 by Brown University student Williams Latham. He wrote of three incidents of baseball being played on the Commons at Brown. The first entry was on Monday, March 9, with another on March 22 and the last on April 9.

Monday 9. We this morning...have been playing ball, But I never have received so much pleasure from it here as I have in Bridgewater. They do not have more than 6 or 7 on a side, so that a great deal of time is spent in running after the ball, Neither do they throw so fair ball, They are afraid the fellow in the middle will hit it with his bat-stick.

As you stroll through the Van Wickle Gates across from the John Hay Library at Brown University, you might be walking the very grounds on which Williams Latham and his fellow students played baseball almost two hundred years ago.

The next written mention of baseball comes in a story titled "A Village Sketch" that appears in the November 27, 1828 edition of the *Torch Light and Public Adviser* from Hagerstown, Maryland. The article describes the stages through which a young girl living in rural Maryland passes. The following portion of the story, focusing on the six-year-old girl, describes her perseverance and playing baseball. (Note the use of the word "baseball" as opposed to "base ball," which was more commonly used during this time period.)

Than comes a sunburn gypsy of six, beginning to grow tall and thin and to find the cares of the world gathering about her, with a pitcher in one hand, a mop in the other, an old straw bonnet of ambiguous shape, half hiding her tangled hair; a tattered petticoat once green, hanging below an equally tattered cotton frock, once purple; her longing eyes fixed on a game of baseball at the corner of the green hill, she reaches the county store, flings down the mop and pitcher and darts off to her companions quite regardless of the storm of scolding with which the mother follows her runaway steps.

As indicated by the almost "afterthought" references to baseball illustrated above, the game was well rooted in the mid-Atlantic and New England traditions by the 1830s. The Abner Doubleday/Cooperstown myth about the creation of baseball was debunked long ago. The real foundation of modern-day baseball was Cartwright's putting pen to paper and inscribing the rules of the game. There's no doubt in my mind that Cartwright did not simply make up the rules on the spot but rather wrote some version of the rules already in play. What Cartwright did was significant because it produced a standardized set of rules. From this humble beginning, the game took off as a "gentleman's game," gaining popularity as an adult game in the 1850s and then spreading via the Civil War in the 1860s.

The Game Matures on Both the Amateur and Professional Scale

What started as a children's game and a pickup game of young men developed into a sophisticated amateur sport that espoused the virtues of physical exercise and honor. However, it wasn't long before commercialism and professionalism encroached upon the sport. There is strong evidence that players in the early 1860s were paid for their services in New York City by Mayor "Boss" Tweed, who placed them on the city morgue payroll without their actually working there. Perhaps it was thought no one would check up on them in such a place.

By 1866, many teams had players who were compensated with cash or given "ghost" jobs to compete on a factory- or city-sponsored team. By the end of the decade, the ground was fertile for the first full-fledged adventure into pure professional baseball. At the end of the 1868 season, the National Association of Base Ball Players, which governed baseball by default, thought it necessary to separate the professionals from the virtuous amateurs by adopting the following rule:

> *Rule V: The Game*
> *Section 7. All players who play base-ball for money, or shall at any time receive compensation for their services as players, shall be considered professional players; and all others shall be regarded as amateur players.*
> —Dewitt's Baseball Guide, 1869

Haney's Base Ball Book

OF REFERENCE FOR 186S.   Price, 20 cents.

Beadle's Dime Base Ball Player

FOR 186S. Price, 10 cents.

DEWITT'S BASE BALL GUIDE

For 186?.   Price 10 cents.

At the

News Depot of

CLARKE & TILLEY,

apr8   128 Thames-S

An advertisement for "Beadle's Dime Base Ball Player" in the *Newport Mercury*, 1869. *Author's collection.*

The real professionalization of the game came with the Cincinnati Red Stockings, who traveled around the country playing local teams in 1869 and 1870. On May 4, 1869, the Red Stockings played their first game as a professional team and beat the Great Westerns 45–9. This game began an eighty-four-game winning streak that did not end until the following summer, when on June 14, 1870, the Atlantics of New York defeated the Red Stockings 8–7. New York player and future Rhode Islander Joe Start, who would later come to play on the great Providence Grays National League team, played a key role in the defeat by knocking in the tying run in the bottom of the eleventh.

Although the game had been played extensively throughout Rhode Island, including Newport, in the 1850s and early 1860s, it definitely gained notoriety in Rhode Island by the mid- to late 1860s and early '70s. One way to gauge the popularity of baseball during this time is to note when the local press began covering games. Following is an account of the earliest mention of baseball played locally in Rhode Island communities.

Providence: Brown University (1827), Empire Club (1866)
Bristol: Bristols (1866)
Warren: Warrens (1868)
Ashaway: Ashaways (1867)
Wakefield: Star (1867)
Westerly: Emments, Pawcatuck BBC (1867)
Cranston: Athletics (1868)
Pawtucket: Actives, Slaters, Hope & Anchor (1868)
Pascoag: Wide Awakes (1868)
Newport: Newports (1869)
White Rock: Sachems (1871)
Riverside: Riversides (1874)
E. Greenwich: Hoes & Atlas BBC (1875)
Woonsocket: Woonsockets (1875)

It didn't take long for Rhode Islanders to develop an unquenchable thirst for baseball, spurred on by the "cranks" and "fanatics" (fans). By 1875, Rhode Island communities had sponsored 118 teams, including the first professional team: the Rhode Islands.

An ancestor of the Providence Juniors, the Rhode Islands came into being in 1875. To help make the team a financially successful enterprise, a brand-new "state of the art" enclosed ball field (Rhode Island's first) was constructed on Adelaide Avenue, between Broad Street and Elmwood Avenue, in Providence. Adelaide Park seated 1,500 people, and at five hundred feet down the lines, it was sizable for its time. It also contained a grandstand, offered ice cream at a brand-new soda parlor and even came complete with a large oak tree with bleachers built around it, offering shade on hot days. Enclosed (fenced-in) ballparks were the key to the financial success of professional baseball teams, for without an enclosed park, collecting admission from patrons was very difficult. The Rhode Islands team lasted three years and never had a losing record. Certainly, one may consider that the Rhode Islands laid the groundwork for Rhode Island's only National League team, the Providence Grays, who played from 1878 through 1885. For local serious baseball team development in Rhode Island, the Rhode Islands set a high standard for both the support of teams and in the construction of ballparks. This lesson was not lost on Newport as residents also began to develop the sport in their city.

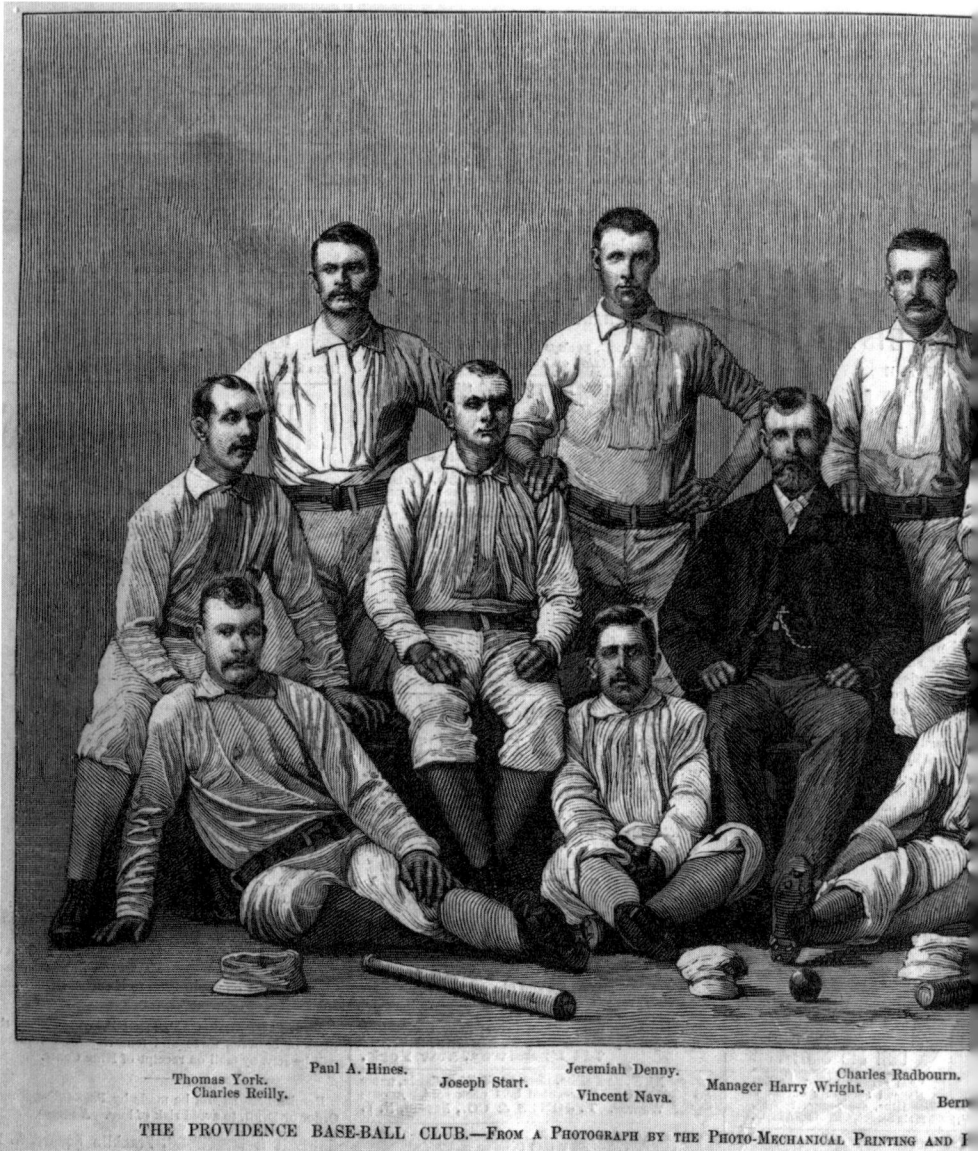

Thomas York. Paul A. Hines. Jeremiah Denny. Charles Radbourn.
Charles Reilly. Joseph Start. Vincent Nava. Manager Harry Wright.
Bern

THE PROVIDENCE BASE-BALL CLUB.—From a Photograph by the Photo-Mechanical Printing and F

A woodcut print of the 1882 Providence Grays from *Harper's Weekly*. *Author's collection.*

Many, including myself, have written about the National League's Providence Grays. In terms of won/loss records, this club was one of the most successful National League franchises ever to have played the game. In its short existence, the team won its first pennant in its second year; won

John Farrell.
'right.   J. M. Ward.

COMPANY, CHICAGO.—[SEE PAGE 619.]

the first World Championship (Series) ever in 1884, beating the New York Metropolitans three games to none in New York City; earned a regular-season record of 488-278 (.637 winning percentage); and had a winning season seven out of eight years. The Grays' only losing season was their last one, and that was due to the financial troubles of the ownership, who sold off some of the team's best players, including the famous pitcher Hoss Radbourn, who had won 59 regular-season games and 3 championship games the previous year. In addition to winning the first world championship, the Providence Grays contributed a number of other baseball "firsts":

• The term "bullpen" was created by the Grays. The bullpen was originally created to park carriages of well-to-do patrons.
• Paul Hines of the Grays was the first player to wear sunglasses during a game and is credited by some researchers with completing the first unassisted triple play in a major-league game. (Accounts of the game involved are not specific.)
• The Grays were the first team to use a turnstile to control fans entering the ballpark.
• On April 30, 1879, Grays pitcher and future Hall of Famer John Ward saved his own shutout by backing up home plate on a throw from the outfield. It was the first recorded instance of this play.
• The Grays' George Wright became the first victim of baseball's reserve system when he turned down Providence's final offer and was not allowed to sign with Worcester.

On the larger scene, baseball was becoming a world commodity. In 1888, Albert Spalding, past professional player and sports equipment czar,

Lou Gehrig Stadium, Yokahama, Japan, circa 1949. *Author's collection.*

organized an around-the-world baseball tour. Originally, the tour was scheduled to visit Australia and was called Spalding's Australian Baseball Tour. But it soon developed into a tour that encompassed Hawaii, New Zealand, Australia, Egypt, France, Italy, Ireland, Scotland and England. Baseball had gone global.

Because of the popularity of baseball spurred on by teams like the Rhode Islands, the Providence Grays, Brown University and many local teams, baseball grew into a spectator and participation sport. The game had become the latest craze being played by just about everyone and in some

odd circumstances also. Baseball had found its way to the most rural areas where sometimes it was even integrated. By mid-century, there were many games and gimmicks associated with baseball.

Back on the home front, Rhode Island communities had sponsored no fewer than 527 teams by 1900, with Newport sponsoring 63 of these. These numbers represent just a fraction of the actual number of teams that I have found to date, and they do not count thousands of local teams not reported on by local newspapers. Baseball was literally being played every day and on just about every open field—whether a diamond had been laid or not—in

PRIMO INCONTRO DELLA NAZIONALE AZZURRA
DI BASEBALL
SPAGNA - ITALIA
STADIO NAZIONALE - ROMA - 31 AGOSTO 1952

"Spagna–Italia." An example of an overseas baseball advertisement demonstrating baseball's international popularity, 1952. *Author's collection.*

Opposite, top: A rare photograph of a rural integrated boys' baseball team, circa 1895. For some communities, baseball could promote equality—at least on the diamond. *Author's collection.*

Opposite, bottom: Rural baseball team, circa 1890. *Author's collection.*

Women playing baseball in Newport, circa 1895. *Courtesy Library of Congress.*

Men playing baseball on Ocean Beach, July 27, 1914. *Courtesy Library of Congress LC-B2-3159-14.*

Above: Royal Arcanum
Society junior state
champions, Newport, circa
1930. *Author's collection.*

Right: A rare King Kelly trading
card, 1888. *Author's collection.*

An advertisement for a game called "Psychic Base Ball," 1949. *Author's collection.*

every community and in every neighborhood. There is no doubt that baseball could claim the number-one entertainment commodity of any community in Rhode Island. By 1900, Newport was on the verge of maturing into a bonanza of baseball that continues today. We will now take a close look at selected Newport teams, players, leagues and ball fields.

Chapter 3
PROFESSIONAL BASEBALL
IN NEWPORT

INTRODUCING THE 1897 NEWPORT COLTS: NEWPORT'S BEST-EVER PROFESSIONAL BASEBALL TEAM

When it comes to professional baseball, Newport has hosted professional teams in only four years. The Newport Colts (1897–99) played in one of the several versions of the New England League. Newport also sported a team in the ill-fated Atlantic Association of 1908. However, when it comes to "rookie" years, Newport's inaugural year in professional ball was quite significant. Not only did the Colts play excellent ball in the 1897 season, but they also shared honors with the Brockton Shoemakers as being the first professional baseball team to tie for a pennant. From 1871 through 1896, there were 136 pennant races, one of which finished in a tie. The Shoemakers and the Colts each finished with a 70-37 record in 1897. According to news accounts of the day, a playoff series did not occur between the two teams because Brockton felt it could be awarded the championship at the next annual meeting and had already discharged its players. Based on Brockton's decision, Newport discharged its players also. In those days, there was little incentive for professional minor-league players to play in a playoff series because no provision had been made to pay them after the regular season—even though the league's bylaws stipulated a playoff series. The league did not rule in Brockton's favor the following year, and the standings and the

HAWLEY, P.	GRANT,	R. F. KELLY, 1b.	GILBERT, C. F.	MILLS, 2 b.
ELLIS, 3 B.	DINSMORE, 3 B.	FINN, MANAGER.	GALLAGHER, P.	PICKECT, L. F.
FOX, P.		BEAN, S. S.	FOLEY, P.	CRISHHAM, C.
Newport News. September 13th, 1897.				

The 1897 Newports, champions of the New England League. *Newport Daily News,* September 13, 1897. *Author's collection.*

tie held. There have been only a handful of pennant ties in the thousands of races since, and most have been settled by a playoff game. There are not many "firsts" in the annals of baseball history, so Newporters can take pride in knowing that their 1897 Colts are part of an answer to a question that most assuredly would stump even the greatest baseball trivia enthusiast: What two teams represent the first tie for a professional league playoff? Answer: The Brockton Shoemakers and the Newport Colts.

The New England League

In 1897, the Class-B New England League was considered a very stable league, having been in operation nine out of eleven years since 1888. The league would be roughly equal to a Double-A league in today's classification system. The 1897 version of the league consisted of six teams: the Newport Colts, the Brockton Shoemakers, the Pawtucket Phenoms, the Fall River Indians, the Taunton Herrings and the New Bedford Whalers. In 1897, all of the league's teams were considered to be in good financial standing, and all had decent to very good home ball fields. Each team played between 105 and 108 games. (The discrepancy of three games played would have been considered a minor problem if standings were not affected. The cost of making up games that would not draw a significant crowd outweighed the need to complete the season in terms of games played.)

The Fall River Indians were heavily favored to win the pennant in 1897. The Indians had entered the league in 1892 and had won four championships in succession (1893–96). Newport was considered a rookie team with no chance of winning. (The last rookie team to win the league's pennant was a Rhode Island team, the 1892 Woonsockets, featuring Hi Ladd, a Rhode Islander who went on to play in the major leagues.) Even though heavily favored in the spring, Fall River found itself in fourth place at the end of the season, with two Rhode Island teams—the Newport Colts and the Pawtucket Phenoms—finishing higher. It would be Rhode Island's best showing ever in the league, which prospered until 1899. That year saw four out of eight teams disband in midseason. The New England League rebounded the following year and lasted through the 1915 season; however, it did not have another Rhode Island team until two resurrections later, in 1946. The 1946 version of the New England League included Rhode Island's Cranston Fire Safes and Pawtucket Slaters. (In 1944, the World War II version of the league boasted a young upstart catcher, Yogi Berra, playing under the name of Joe Canuso.) The New England League went out of existence for good after the 1949 season.

The Newport Colts and the 1897 Season

Newport's excellent season in 1897 can be attributed to three major factors. First, the team was very stable in terms of personnel. The Colts needed to add only three major players during the season, which was done early, and released only Stephenson, the left fielder, who left for personal reasons. Second, the team boasted an excellent pitching staff. Marvin H. Hawley led the league with twenty-four wins, and Andrew Gallagher and Patrick Foley were very consistent as well. All three pitchers made it through the season without major injury. The rotation of Hawley, Gallagher and Foley was considered far superior to that of any other team in the league, according to news accounts of the day. Third, the Colts played excellent defense and posted a respectable .277 batting average. Newport outscored its opponents by an average of 1.5 runs per game (6.0 runs scored by Newport versus 4.5 runs by opponents).

Personnel

The talent on the '97 Colts team was impressive and a tribute to the team's small but effective "front office." The foundation of the team was actually developed in 1896, when five players and the manager were signed. All of the players possessed some level of professional experience. Most of the players came from New England, as the league's charter directed teams to engage players primarily from the New England area. Only three Newport players came from outside New England: one from Ohio, one from New Jersey and one from Pennsylvania. Six members of the squad had played in the majors or would play there in the future. Four players hit over .300, led by David Pickett at .339. Pickett was followed by Patrick Crisham (.316), Joseph Bean (.316) and Michael Kelly (.309). The pitching, as stated earlier, was outstanding by the standards of the time. Following are short biographical sketches of the main players.

Michael J. Flynn, manager: Flynn came to the team in 1896 and continued as manager until 1899. He had served in Minneapolis in 1888–89 under the tutelage of manager P.T. Powers, who later became president of the Eastern (International) League. In 1889–90, he was with the All-American team that toured the world. Flynn then engaged in newspaper work in Boston until he signed on with the Newports.

Michael J. Kelly, first base and captain: From Otter River, Massachusetts, Kelly started with the New England League's Augusta team as a catcher and then transitioned to first base in 1895–96. He signed with Newport for the '97 season.

Joseph W. Bean, shortstop: From Cambridge, Massachusetts, Bean played for Augusta in 1895 and 1896. During the winter season, he was a gymnasium instructor in Cambridge. Bean played forty-eight games with the New York Giants in 1902.

Patrick J. Crisham, catcher: In 1895, Crisham, a native of Amesbury, Massachusetts, played for New England League clubs at Lowell and Lewiston. Lewiston released him due to a leg injury. He signed with Newport in 1896. Crisham played one year in the majors (Baltimore, 1899).

Albert Dinsmore, third base/shortstop: From Stamford, Connecticut, Dinsmore began his baseball career playing for the Detroit Free Press team, champion of the Newsboys' League. In 1895, he played for the Young Men's Christian Association team of Detroit before signing with Newport in 1896.

Benjamin Ellis, third base/shortstop: From New York City, Ellis began his professional career with Pottsville of the Pennsylvania State League (1894–95). He played in four games with the Philadelphia Athletics in 1896 and began the '97 season in Detroit before being moved to New Bedford and, finally, Newport.

Patrick Foley, pitcher/shortstop: From Fitchburg, Massachusetts, Foley played with a semipro independent Orange, Massachusetts team in 1896 before signing with Newport in 1897.

Andrew T. Gallagher, pitcher/right field: From Amsterdam, New York, Gallagher began his career with the Allentown, Pennsylvania Young Men's Christian Association in 1890. He then pitched for Lehigh University in 1891–92 and moved to the Williamsport (Pennsylvania) Trade Nine in '93. Gallagher returned to college ball, playing for Union College in 1895, and then pitched for his hometown Amsterdam entry in the New York State League in '96 before signing with Newport for the 1897 season.

John R. Gilbert, center field: From Albany, New York, Gilbert improved his baseball prowess with the Albany Newsboy team that finished in second place in 1893. In 1894, he played for Albany of the New York State League, and in '95 he played for both Nashua and Lewiston of the New England League. He signed with Newport in 1896. Gilbert played for the Washington Senators and New York Giants in 1898 and for the Pittsburgh Pirates in 1904.

George W. Grant, right field/catcher/second base: From Taunton, Massachusetts, Grant broke into professional baseball with the independent New Bedford team of 1893–94. In '95, he patrolled the outfield with Lowell of the New England League before signing with Newport in '96.

Marvin H. Hawley, pitcher/right field: From Conneaut, Ohio, Hawley pitched for Oberlin College in 1894 before spending three weeks with the Boston Beaneaters of the National League. He signed with Toledo of the Western League in 1895 and was farmed to Lowell, later returning to Toledo. He spent the '96 season with Springfield of the Eastern League and signed with Newport in 1897.

Samuel Mills, second base: Easton, Pennsylvania native Mills began his professional career with Evansville of the Southern League in 1887. Prior to 1892, he also played with New Orleans and Mobile. He then returned home to play with Easton of the Pennsylvania League for the 1892-93 seasons before moving to Grand Rapids of the Western League in 1895. He started the '97 season with Wilkes-Barre (Eastern League) and then switched to Newport.

David T. Pickett, left field: Pickett hailed from Brookline, Massachusetts, and had played for Lowell (1894) and Augusta (1895–96) of the New England League. He went on to play for the major league Boston Nationals in 1898.

The Colts made one big mistake in their final year, 1899, when they passed up a kid fresh out of Newport's Rogers High School. That kid was Frank Corridon, who later played in the majors and is credited with inventing the spitball.

SUMMARY OF THE COLTS: 1897–99

The Colts had a great 1897 season, playing steadily and professionally all summer. They led the league in wins for all but three weeks in the spring. Their pitching was stellar and their offense effective. As a team, the Colts led the league in many defensive categories. It must have been a wonderful time to be a baseball fan in Newport. The economy was recovering from a severe depression, the hope and promise of a new technologically oriented century was just on the horizon and Newport's first professional baseball team was top-shelf. Although the season ended in a controversial tie, Newporters must have been ecstatic regarding the play of their home team. But they had no way of knowing that the season would have to suffice as the best season Newport could boast.

The 1898 season did not prove to be as enjoyable, as the Colts finished two games under .500 and in fourth place. The '99 season, however, proved to be interesting. According to the record books, the Colts finished six games over .500 and in third place. Newporters and the local press saw it very differently, and Newport was once again in the center of controversy. The season started out with eight teams: the Colts, the Portland Phenoms, the Manchester Manchesters, the Taunton Herrings, the Brockton Shoemakers, the Pawtucket Colts, Fitchburg/Lawrence and Cambridge. By May 24, Fitchburg had moved to Lawrence, and by June 1, both Lawrence and Cambridge had disbanded. On August 8, Brockton and Pawtucket followed suit, leaving only four teams to finish the season. The demise of half the teams left the question of the league championship very much up in the air. Modern record books include all eight teams when determining league final standings. However, local press accounts of the period demonstrate a very different perspective.

The remaining teams in the league decided to divide the season into halves, each with its own set of standings. The pennant was to go to the winner of the second-half season in what was called the "supplemental series." Here is where it gets a little confusing. In the second half of the season, Newport won twenty-two games and lost nine. If only these games were to be counted, Newport would have finished in first place. The controversy arose when both Newport and Manchester played—and won—three and six games, respectively, on the last day of the season. Two of the additional games won by Manchester were challenged by Newport. It is not clear whether the issue was ever officially resolved by the league. In the greater scheme of things, perhaps the actual official league standings are not that important. However, the news account that appeared in the September 5, 1899 edition of the *Newport News* best explains the particulars of the controversial situation and is a fitting end to this chapter.

BASE BALL SEASON ENDED
Newport and Manchester Both Claim the Supplementary Series

The supplementary season of the New England League baseball clubs was concluded yesterday, so far as the playing is concerned, but there is likely to be considerable talk regarding the claims of both clubs for the championship. The Newports played three games yesterday with the Tauntons, which were regarded as necessary to complete the schedule between the two. Manchester and Portland clubs played five games and started a sixth, which was awarded to Manchester because the Portland manager refused to allow one of his players to be put out of the game. It is claimed by Newport that there were no postponed games between these clubs and that two of the games were all they had a right to play in the regular schedule, to complete the series.

The Newports won their three games and claim that they have thus taken the championship pennant. The Manchesters also won all the games they played, and these victories would give them the lead in the race. If the two games are allowed Newport will win, but if all the Manchester victories are allowed Manchester is ahead. It is a peculiar state of things that allows two clubs to play all the games they wish on the closing day, and it is doubtful if Manchester's claim will be allowed. The final decision will probably come from the board of arbitration of the National League, under which the New England League has been operated.

THE ATLANTIC ASSOCIATION AND THE 1908 PONIES: NEWPORT'S LAST ATTEMPT AT PROFESSIONAL BALL
Newport First

The Newport Ponies were one of three Rhode Island teams that signed up for the short-lived Atlantic Association. There were three other teams in the league, two from Maine and one from Massachusetts. Newport was thrilled to engage in organized baseball once more. The following account of the league's Opening Day was published in the May 4, 1908 edition of the *Newport Daily News*:

The Atlantic Association season opened in Newport Saturday at Wellington Park under fairly satisfactory weather conditions. The weather had been threatening and unpleasant until past noon, but then the sun came out— and so did the cranks and dyed-in-the-wool baseball enthusiasts—and filled the park. The bleachers overflowed early, the grandstand was packed, the spectators stood as deep along the infield fence as they could and even spread out in a flanking movement for a good view, until the left foul line

Unknown team at Wellington Park, circa 1920. *Courtesy George Donnelly Jr.*

almost reached the fence. If the estimated seating capacity of the stands was correct, there were 2,000 people present. There are reasons to believe that the estimated capacity was less than announced and that the total attendance was less. Still it could be called a big crowd.

There was a parade before the game. Headed by the Newport Military Band, the two teams in drags proceeded to the ball grounds, with Mayor Clarke and officials [illegible] a local club and an accompanying carriage. Arriving at the grounds they found them well filled already, with more waiting to buy tickets. The teams at once began practice, the visitors starting. They were a big-looking set up of players, but did nothing startling. Then the Newports did some fielding work, and it was noticed that Manager Henry was in uniform and went out in the field and showed that he could still do the trick. The visitors wore a white uniform with red trimmings and stockings; it looked pretty, but some of the suits looked dirty, the inevitable result of playing real base ball in such colors. The Newport uniforms of grey with blue trimmings were neat as to color and much enduring an appearance, not needing attention from the laundry every time a player slid for a base. The band played at intervals, and the grandstand filled up and the crowd grew larger on either foul line.

It was four o'clock, the hour for the game to start. Both teams lined up in front of the home plate facing the grandstand, and President Anthony of the Newport club introduced president Hugh McBreen of the Atlantic Association and Mayor Clarke. The mayor spoke briefly, saying this was the first meeting of the Atlantic League, and all Newporters seemed to be wishing the Newport team all the good luck it could have. They also desired to see good playing, and that the team should play fast, clean ball...

There was one thing which especially pleased the crowd, and that was that Patty Martin showed he was not lost in the shuffle. Instead of being lost, he shone brightly as he took in two dives which called for judgment in running and were the two best catches of the game, and he broke the ice by making the first hit of the game.

All seemed to be set for a great baseball season for the new league. Five of the six host cities had a history of supporting minor-league baseball at higher levels, and there was no reason to expect that there would be a problem with this Class C minor league. The Atlantic Association included the Portland Blue Sox (Maine), the Lewistons (Maine), the Pawtucket Colts (Rhode Island), the Taunton Angels (Massachusetts), the Woonsocket Trotters (Rhode Island) and the Newport Ponies. Newport was selected to host the opening game of the league. No one in the enthusiastic crowd that day could have predicted that ten games later, the Atlantic Association would no longer exist. To understand what happed to the ill-fated circuit, one must look at the environment in which it was created. As it turns out, the world of baseball was a wild and free-swinging entity.

The Atlantic Association (February 20, 1908–May 21, 1908)

The era of the late 1940s and early 1950s is often referred to as the "Golden Age" of the minor leagues. Organized baseball reached the apex of fifty-nine leagues in 1949. However, the real Golden Age, which also accounts for amateur and semipro organizations, would have to be the first seventeen years of the twentieth century: 1900–16. Not only did the period see the development of the American League (1901), the birth and death of the Federal League (1914–15) and forty-nine minor leagues in operation by 1910, but every American city, town and neighborhood played host to amateur and semipro teams. Major populated areas had semipro and amateur industrial/mill leagues playing full schedules and drawing upward of five thousand fans at games. Major leaguers often supplemented their paltry salaries by playing in the industrial leagues or for town-sponsored semipro teams. Some of these players even forfeited their major-league contracts or played under assumed names because they could make more money in these leagues. There was ample opportunity even in the smallest dust speck on the roadmap to sponsor one or more teams.

During this time, the term "amateur" was also tested, with many players receiving "ghost" jobs in factories or money under the table. Amateur teams openly discussed the "signing" of out-of-towners to play on the local team. As early as 1895, towns like Pascoag threatened to run their "amateur" teams out of town due to the rough character of the players, who, after all, "weren't from town at all," according to the *Pascoag Herald*. Fighting, drinking and gambling were listed as some of the less-desired attributes of players on Pascoag's "amateur" team. The gambling by players sometimes even extended into the games themselves. Even the prestigious and long-running amateur Tim O'Neil League of Providence (1901–51) included nonlocal minor-league players "between baseball jobs" sprinkled throughout the league during the early years. I have interviewed several players from the league who, with a wink, hinted that they knew of some players who received money in exchange for their talents. Even colleges weren't immune. One elder Rhode Island resident remembers his father being paid to play for a prestigious local college team as an "anonymous ringer" in important games during seasons in the early 1920s.

Also on the local Rhode Island scene, the Palace Gardens in Lakewood (Warwick) was in full swing, playing illegally on the Sabbath with as many as eight amateur and semipro games being played simultaneously. (During the 1920s, liquor was openly sold at these games despite Prohibition, with several incidents of the constables being called in because of drunken and rowdy teenagers.) In 1908, Rhode Island alone sported many leagues. (Newport was one of several Rhode Island cities in which baseball was played illegally on Sundays.) On the amateur level, besides the Tim O'Neil League, every social institution and profession sponsored their own league. There were several church leagues, lawyers' leagues, clerks' leagues, policemen and firefighters' leagues and regional industrial leagues. Every town sponsored at least one independent amateur or semipro team. The Class-A Providence Grays were in their heyday, playing at the newly constructed Melrose Park. (A plaque can be found installed by the Society for American Baseball Research at the former location of Melrose Park commemorating Babe Ruth's play in 1914 at this park when he was a member of the pennant-winning Grays.) The most prominent semipro league was the Mill League, anchored in Woonsocket. (As will be demonstrated, the Woonsocket Mill League played a prominent role in the demise of the Trotters and ultimately started the chain of actions that brought down the Atlantic Association.)

The result of all this baseball within the small confines of Rhode Island's borders in 1908 was competition for the entertainment dollar. As popular as baseball was, lack of "spending money" for the everyday working family would also play a key role in the demise of the Atlantic League. The Rhode Island and New England economy was based on industry. There certainly were wealthy people living in Rhode Island, but the largest segment of the population was by far first- or second-generation immigrants who worked long and often-dangerous hours in factories and mills, including many women and children who were full-time employees in the mills. It would be an understatement to say that the "entertainment dollar" was stretched very thin. On any day of the week, there were literally dozens of amateur, semipro or professional games being played in Rhode Island, and most charged a fee to watch. To be a financially successful ballclub, the organization needed to compete for the entertainment dollar that, in turn, competed with money needed for rent, food and clothing. Rhode Island was not a wealthy community. Not only was money in short supply, but with the workers' long hours, time and energy were also in short supply. Despite these dire circumstances, most teams thrived, and workers still found energy to play the nation's sport.

Out of this conglomeration of early baseball arose the Atlantic League. In hindsight, and with an understanding of the realities of economic competition and several other factors, one would have been able to advise the principals of the league to not even entertain the idea of starting the Atlantic Association. The league was born, however, and it was laid to rest after only three weeks of playing life. In addition to the competition for the entertainment dollar, there were sociological factors that contributed to the fate of the Atlantic Association. Sometimes outcomes are not guided by our own efforts but rather the result of factors beyond our control. There is no indication that the city of Newport (which apparently even built a new ball field to host its team), the owners of Newport Ponies, the Newport players or the fans had anything to do with the demise of their beloved team. In reality, Newport very likely could have sustained a minor-league team for years to come if the league had continued. The team had no real competition other than a semipro team called the Newports, which had been around for a couple decades. There certainly was enough capital in the thriving city to support the team. However, the fate of the Newport Ponies was intricately linked to the fate of the other host cities and to the way the league was organized. Unlike Newport, the other five host cities faced stiff competition from the Mill/Industrial Leagues. The significance of this factor is best demonstrated later in this section by the story of the Woonsocket Trotters, the first to fall. (Author's note: The Woonsocket Trotters hold the distinction of being the only professional team to have a losing record without ever playing game. How is this possible? To find out, read on.)

Birth of the Atlantic Association: An Optimistic Beginning

The news of the birth of the Atlantic Association broke on February 20 simultaneously in newspapers all across the country. The typical announcement is reflected in a short article in the March 17, 1908 *Syracuse Herald*:

> ### ATLANTIC ASSOCIATION
> *New Baseball League Formally Organizes at Boston*
>
> *Boston. The Atlantic Baseball Association was formally organized in the city yesterday. The circuit was decided upon as follows: Lewiston, Maine; Portland, Maine; Newport, Rhode Island; Pawtucket, Rhode Island; Woonsocket, Rhode Island; and Taunton, Massachusetts. It was voted to open the season May 2 and end September 7. Hugh McBreen was elected president, and Fred Lake, formerly of the National and New England Leagues, was chosen as secretary-treasurer.*

A quick media search resulted in finding the above posting in every major newspaper—including the *New York Times* and the *Washington Post*—as well as small-market papers. Several of these papers reported that the association agreed that no team would exceed a $1,000-a-month salary. (Historical note: Fred Lake, besides being a major-league player with the Boston Red Sox and Boston Doves (Braves), was a scout and is credited with the discovery of Rhode Island native and Hall of Famer Nap Lajoie.)

THE NEWPORT PONIES: FIRST GAME

Newport was chosen to play the first game of the Atlantic Association schedule. The city had built Wellington Park for the Ponies. A great crowd came to watch their home team play the Lewistons. As it turned out, if there were any Lewiston fans in the crowd, they would have gone home much happier than did the Newport fans. Newport batters struggled against Lewiston's pitcher, Merrill. Brown, the pitcher for Newport, at least did not embarrass himself, giving up nine hits and four runs. Newport was able to muster only two hits and did not score any runs. The crowd was happy about one thing, however: local favorite Paddy Martin had one of the hits and had two excellent defensive plays in right field. The reporter for the *Newport Daily News* was particularly satisfied with the calling of Umpire Reagan. The game lasted one hour and thirty-seven minutes. Readers today would find this time frame amazing, but at the turn of the twentieth century, very few games lasted more than an hour and a half. (Historical note: The quality of umpiring in the early 1900s for low-level minor-league games was definitely suspect, and it was unusual to have a well-called game. During this time period, umpiring was also not a particularly safe occupation, with crowds at times taking matters into their own hands. Just twenty-four years earlier, in a major-league game played by the Kansas City Cowboys of the Union

Players speeding up the umpire, 1885. *Author's collection.*

How would you like to be the Umpire?

A humorous cartoon involving an umpire, circa 1907. *Author's collection.*

Association in Kansas City in 1884, Buffalo Bill Cody was called on to umpire a game after the umpire the previous day had been severely injured by an unruly and unhappy crowd. By the way, in this game, the Kansas City second baseman was Rhode Islander and former Brown University star Charlie Bassett. In Buffalo Bill's game, a fan started to lose control, and according to the *Kansas City Star*, Buffalo Bill drew his pistol and shot the man's hat off. Subsequent reports by the *Star* stated that the Cowboys experienced no more problems from fans for the rest of the season.)

THE PONIES' SEASON

For the next three weeks, the Newporters played hard, if not decently. They took the second game of the season in a 6–5 over Lewiston, with Mulvey pitching for Newport and Irish pitching for Lewiston. Paddy Martin had two hits. In contrast, the Ponies' third game, against the Portland Blue Sox, was a slugfest. Portland had eleven hits and scored 9 runs, while Newport had nine hits and scored 7 runs. McGrady pitched for Portland and Clarke for Newport. The fourth game was even more of a slugfest, with 22 runs being scored by the two teams. The Ponies' opponent was the Attleboro

Angels, formally the Taunton Angels, who had switched host cities the first week of the season (another troubling sign for the league). Payne pitched for the Newports, giving up 12 runs and taking the loss, while Attleboro pitcher Wilson gave up 10 runs for the win. On May 9, it was reported that the vacancy left by Woonsocket still had not been filled.

Waiting for their next opponent, the Ponies took on the Seamen Gunners from the Newport navy station. The Ponies won easily, 14–0, with Mulvey pitching. The next league game, against the Pawtucket Colts, was played to a 7–7 tie, called because of darkness. On May 13, Newport once again squared off against Pawtucket and lost. This time they lost 9–6, Sanford pitching for Pawtucket and Walsh for Newport. Newport's record now stood at one win and four losses. Martin continued his hot hitting with three hits in the game. By the third inning of the sixth game, things were not looking good for the home team. Portland led 6–0. However, Newport rallied and wound up the victor in an 8–6 score. Right fielder Paddy Martin went four for four. After six games, Martin was batting .414, third best in the league, and was leading the league with 12 runs. He was also fielding 1.000.

On May 18, Newport played another exhibition game, this time with the Marines, winning 2–0. One day later, Newport began to turn things around, beating Attleboro 8–1 behind the good pitching of Mulvey. Paddy Martin went two for four. On May 19, Newport beat Attleboro 11–2 behind Coffey's pitching. Martin again went two for four. However, the headline for the game read: "LEWISTON TEAM DESERTED BY MANAGER BEADE." The erosion of the Atlantic Association was now in full swing. On May 19, the Pawtucket Colts disbanded. On May 20, playing at Wellington Grounds, Newport pitcher Welch shut out Lewiston 3–0, with the *Newport Daily News* still providing excellent coverage of the games. At that time, neither team realized that it had just played the last game of the Atlantic Association.

IT STARTED IN NEWPORT AND ENDED IN NEWPORT

Following is the *Newport Daily News'* May 22, 1908 report of last game played in the Atlantic Association League:

> *The balloon ascension in which the Atlantic Association went up in the air yesterday must have included Mobley and most of the Newport team, for the exhibition they gave Thursday afternoon in the last game of the league was*

certainly of that kind. With Mulvey in the box, a steady exhibition patient was looked for, but it was not forthcoming. He was banged around safely, and banged against and over the fence. Then the fielders had a case of cold feet, and could not hold the ball when they got their handle on it, and did not try to get their hands on it at other times, so that, taken all in all, it was by far the worst showing the team has made. Yet there were bright moments after an exhibition by the outfielder Sullivan, who would get into the game and for an instant, and it could be seen that Newport could play. On the other side, Lewiston did not seem at all affected by the balloon ascension and played steady ball, and batting hard and fielding perfectly made a record by playing two consecutive games without an error.

Newport lost to Lewiston 7–1 the last game ever played in the Atlantic Association. Why did the Atlantic Association fail? I'm sure the organizers of the league looked at the vast experience of the combined cities chosen in professional organized baseball. Portland had twelve years of minor-league ball. Lewiston had seven years. Pawtucket had seven years, Taunton four years, Newport three years and Woonsocket two years. All cities had a long history of strong amateur and semipro baseball dating to the late 1860s, and all sported decent ball fields. Five of the six cities had one factor in common: they all had large industrial-based mill teams and leagues. Only Newport had a different economic base, with a much smaller percentage of its economic activity centered on industrial settings and a much larger base that included services related to the tourist industry, shipping activities, areas of high real-estate value and a base of support from wealthy summer visitors. It also had a strong city government, which invested in recreational activities for residents.

Perhaps the best way to sum up the demise of the Atlantic Association is with an article that appeared in the May 23, 1908 edition of the *Newport Mercury*:

The Atlantic Association of baseball clubs has been shipwrecked before getting out of the home port. It has been learned that several of the original teams will be unable to go on and the schedule has been suspended, probably not to be reinstated.

The Atlantic Association was organized in the early spring. The cities represented were Newport, Taunton, Woonsocket, Attleboro, Lewiston, and Portland. The first team to die a natural death was Woonsocket, which found no support in the hometown, owing to the popularity of the Mill League. Then Attleboro succumbed, and this week Pawtucket deemed it advisable to withdraw, which marked the end of the league.

When the league was started, Newporters rejoiced to see professional baseball resume in their city after a lapse of several years. The indications were that the local team would receive good support when the summer came, and although the Newports had not developed a team of unusual strength, they played good ball to good audiences. Demonstrating the local support for high quality baseball, the city's residents showed enough interest that a team was continued even after the Atlantic Association collapsed, as indicated the following excerpt from the *Newport Mercury*:

> *Just what will be done with the local team is a matter not yet decided. The stockholders will have a meeting in Mercury Hall on Saturday evening for the purpose of talking over matters and taking decisive action. It seems likely that the players will be retained here and the club will go on independent of any league. There are several strong amateur teams in this vicinity, and opportunity will frequently arise to meet the professional teams of the Eastern or New England Leagues. The local organization has excellent grounds, and many think it will be a mistake to let slip the present opportunity to have professional baseball here.*

In other Atlantic Association cities, most players left to pursue other opportunities. In Newport certainly some players left, but the team continued to have a successful summer season as an independent professional team. The following year would see the development of (in the author's opinion) the most successful semipro team anywhere: the Trojans.

Chapter 4
SIGNIFICANT TEAMS

THE TROJANS: THE BEST SEMIPRO BASEBALL TEAM

The Trojans are by far the greatest semi professional team this researcher has ever found. The team organized in 1908, played its first official game in 1909 and continued through 1922 (with the exception of the war year of 1918). During this time, the Trojans amassed a total of 195 wins, 56 losses and 3 ties for a winning percentage of .777. They scored a total of 1,198 runs and gave up only 672 for a run differential of 526. Anyone who has knowledge of baseball history and follows the sport today knows that statistics don't come close to telling the entire story; however, these are pretty impressive numbers. I have come up with a formula to determine just how good a nineteenth- or twentieth-century semiprofessional team was. The important factors include:

1. Quality of the field allotted to the team.
2. Attendance.
3. Press coverage by local daily and weekly papers.
4. Strength of opponents.
5. Number of games played in the season.
6. Number of minor-league/major-league teams played.
7. Level of professional experience of players.
8. Ratio of home games to away games.
9. Statistical analysis, especially won/loss ratios.

There are many factors that affect the length of a team's existence that are not controlled by the team. For this reason, I do not take this factor into consideration. By all the above measures, the Trojans outdistance any of the other semiprofessional teams I have explored.

For the majority of the Trojans' existence, the best field in Newport was Wellington Grounds, which had been built specifically for the professional Atlantics in 1908. Because of the demise of the Atlantics, the field became available. Although the Trojans were a newly formed team, the city of Newport saw it fit to lease the field to the Trojans despite many other good teams of the time. For all intents and purposes, the Trojans owned the best field in Newport almost until their end. Throughout the years of play, the Trojans were always number one in attendance. In both the *Newport Daily News* and the *Newport Mercury*, the most covered team was the Trojans, with generous multicolumn coverage for almost every game. In addition, the papers often provided pregame coverage with full analysis of teams to be played.

The Trojans played primarily the best teams available, including major-league teams, minor-league teams and semipro teams from Massachusetts, Connecticut and Rhode Island. They tended to play only the best army and navy teams stationed in Newport. The Trojans carried a heavy schedule every season, with most seasons topping over twenty games. This is significant given the fact that every player had a day job. In any given year, the roster included players with professional experience. Many of the Trojans players were recruited by minor-league professional teams, and they were often scouted by major-league scouts representing franchises from New York and Boston. The vast majority of games played were home games. This is a key factor when determining the strength and relevance of a semiprofessional baseball team. The last factor in deciding the significance of the semiprofessional team is a statistical analysis. As demonstrated in the first paragraph in this discussion about the Trojans, nothing more need be said relating to the outstanding accomplishments statistically of this team.

Common lore places the responsibility of development of the Trojans with a group of men who attended grammar school together and to one man in particular. According to George Donnelly Jr., Alan Langley was the

Opposite, top: The Trojans in their new uniforms, 1908. *Courtesy George Donnelly Jr.*

Opposite, bottom: A Braves contemporary with the Trojans, circa 1910. *Courtesy George Donnelly Jr.*

William West, Trojans player and one-time commissioner of the Sunset League. *Courtesy George Donnelly Jr.*

guiding light and genius behind developing the Trojans. Another significant figure was William West.

Right from the start, the Trojans establish themselves as a team to be reckoned with. In their first year (1909), they won 6 games and lost only 2. In 1910, they sported a 10–0 record. Although the Trojans had many great players, it is hard to beat the performance of their best pitcher, Sheehan, who won 57 games against 8 losses in his career with the Trojans. That computes to a .877 winning percentage, which would be tough to beat in any league at any level. One must remember that during this time, pitchers almost always completed their own games, making a high number of wins even more remarkable. Sheehan had seven consecutive winning years for the Trojans; however, the 1910 (9-0) and 1914 (10-0) seasons were his most outstanding.

Two Rhode Island native major leaguers played for the Trojans at different times. One, native Newporter Frank Corridon, has a write-up in this book. The other is Cranston native Jimmy Cooney of baseball's famous Cooney family. He played several games, and we have a record of what he was paid for one of them: seven dollars. The Cooney family was all about baseball. Issues of the *Cranston Herald* from the 1920s contain many box scores of nine members of the Cooney family playing for significant teams—and winning! However, of significance to the professional baseball world, four Cooneys are relevant. It starts with the patriarch, James Joseph Cooney, who was born in Cranston in 1865. The elder James played fifteen years of professional ball, including three years in the National League for the Chicago Cubs and the Washington Senators. Unfortunately, he died early at age thirty-eight—but not before passing on the baseball bug to all of his many sons, especially Jimmy and Johnny. Jimmy "Scoops" Edward Cooney, the Cooney who played for the Trojans, was born in 1894. He was the first of the clan to join the pro baseball ranks, signing on with the Worcester club of the New England League in 1913. All told, he played twenty years of professional ball, including seven seasons in the major leagues. Next up was John "Johnny" Walter Cooney Sr., who was born in 1901. Johnny, as he was known, played twenty-five years of professional ball and was by far the most successful in the major leagues, where he played twenty of those years. Johnny was one of those rare individuals who started as a pitcher, became injured and after thirteen years switched to the outfield and played another twelve years. As of the writing of this book, the last baseball Cooney was James William Cooney, who was born to Jimmy in 1920. He played for four minor-league seasons: 1939–41 and 1946. He spent 1942–45 in military service.

In honor of the Trojan dynasty, following are short summaries of the first and last games played by the team. The first one took place on March 27, 1909, against the Hiltons. The headlines read, "Yield to the Trojans: Hiltons Suffered Their Second Baseball Defeat of the Season, by 9–4 Score." In the Trojans' first official game, they displayed good offense, collecting fourteen hits, and fair pitching by left-hander Beattie, who gave up 4 runs. The team committed no errors. The stars on offense were Debois, Morley and J. McGowan, who each had three hits. The Hiltons were a well-known semipro team of high caliber. It was a good start for the Trojans.

The last recorded game for the Trojans came on October 1, 1922, against the Fall River Legion, a semiprofessional team. The Trojans ended their legacy just as they had begun it—with a win. The Trojans took the game

Left: Jimmy Cooney, circa 1926.
Author's collection.

Below: An entry from the Trojans' record book showing a payout to Jimmy Cooney, 1913.
Courtesy George Donnelly Jr.

7–3 behind the pitching of Berry. They had ten hits to Legion's five, with Monrganroth, Callahan and Berry each getting two hits. The pitcher for Fall River, Golden, had pitched for the Trojans in previous years. (It was not an uncommon practice for players, especially pitchers, on semiprofessional teams to switch allegiances sometimes within the same week. They tended to go where the money and opportunity was.) There is a small mystery concerning the end of the Trojans. The news account indicates that this game was to be the first of a series to establish a championship. The Trojans had been covered well all season by both papers; however, there were no more reports of games after this one in either paper. Thus, we are left with having no knowledge of whether the games were ever played.

So ends a brief telling of the Trojans' story. Truly, a future author might consider writing a book solely about this team. There certainly is enough material.

Salve Regina University

Salve Regina University, founded by the Sisters of Mercy, was originally chartered by the State of Rhode Island in 1937. After receiving a donation in 1947 from the Robert Walton Goelet estate, which included Ocher Court (a Newport mansion abutting the Cliff Walk), the school welcomed its first class of 58 students. Over the years, the university has grown considerably, being careful to stay small enough to offer an intimate learning experience. It now serves over 2,600 undergraduate and graduate students and also offers a small doctoral program. The students enjoy one of the most stunningly beautiful campuses on the Atlantic seaboard. The eighty-acre university grounds contain many historic buildings, mansions and even converted stables that once housed riding horses belonging to the wealthy individuals who summered in Newport.

Baseball at Salve: A Short Synopsis

Like the university itself, baseball at Salve is comparatively new to the college ranks. However, the sport has grown into a mature endeavor, and Salve has won an impressive number of games in its young history. Since its inaugural season of 1981, the Seahawks have amassed a record of 579 wins against 443 losses and 4 ties for a .566 winning percentage. This record is especially notable considering the team did not have a winning record for the first seven seasons, which is to be expected considering the infancy of the program. The Seahawks have won the Commonwealth Coast League (CCC) championship seven times, qualified for the CCC playoffs nine times, gone to the NCAA Division III championship twice and appeared in the Eastern College Athletic Conference (ECAC) championship twice.

Throughout the years, Salve Regina University baseball players have set a number of conference and national records. The 2012–13 season demonstrates the trend developing in more recent play. In this season, the Seahawks went 29-12, boasted six all-conference selections, had a freshman player named CCC Rookie of the Year and had players selected for the First and Second Team All New England. In twelve offensive categories, the team also finished in the top fifteen nationally.

Salve Regina University is a founding member of the Commonwealth Coast Conference, which was established in 1984 and is affiliated with the NCAA's Division III. There are currently ten colleges in the league. Because Salve Regina is a Division III school, no athletic scholarships can be offered, which makes recruiting baseball players a huge job for the coaches. On the flip side, players do not have to worry about maintaining baseball scholarships and are able to concentrate more on having fun, as well as honing their baseball skills. That is not to say, however, that the players are not serious about their game; nothing can be further from the truth. No team can win so consistently without taking competition and the game seriously, and several of the players have gone on to sign minor-league contracts or play in competitive summer amateur leagues.

What makes a good team is not only good players but also the coaching staff and strong support from the university. Salve Regina University strongly supports its sports teams and can boast many championships among their sports programs. The school has supported baseball by hiring experienced and strong coaches. There have been five head coaches at Salve, two of which will be highlighted in this book. Following are the names of the head coaches, the years in which they coached and their won/loss records:

Coach	Years at Salve Regina	Won/Loss Record	Winning Percentage
Mike Chadwick	1981–82	7-24	.225
Paul Gamache	1983–84	14-22	.388
Andy Andrade	1985–99	240-164-2	.594
Steve Cirella	2000–13	318-233-2	.577
Eric Cirella	2014	N/A	N/A

Eric Cirella, head baseball coach at Salve Regina University, 2014. *Photo credit author.*

Meet the Cirellas: Steve and Eric

Meet Salve Regina University's newest and fifth head coach, Eric Cirella. Coach Cirella has traveled many miles in his young baseball career and follows in his father's footsteps as head coach at Salve. Cirella was associate coach for Salve Regina University in 2012–13 prior to being named head coach. However, I'm letting the story get ahead of us. Eric Cirella was born on July 6, 1982, in Jamestown, Rhode Island, and grew up in a baseball household. Eric's story actually starts with his father, Steve Cirella, and Steve's story must be told first.

Coach Steve Cirella: Longtime Baseball Man

Steve Cirella played baseball and football in college while at Amherst and possesses a very significant baseball résumé. Besides his fourteen-year career as head coach of the Salve Regina University baseball team, Steve Cirella served as coach for Coventry High School, the American Legion and the George Donnelly Sunset League. As coach at Salve Regina, Cirella's teams won twenty-plus games in eleven of fourteen seasons and in 2006 set a school record with thirty-two wins. As head coach, he led the Seahawks to two conference championships and twice took them to the ECAC playoffs, capturing the title in 2004. Cirella's Seahawks also advanced to the NCAA Tournament twice. During his tenure at Salve, Cirella also accumulated a number of accolades. He was twice named CCC Coach of the Year, and he was named to the Rhode Island Baseball Coaches Association Hall of Fame in 2011. As of this writing, Mr. Cirella is the director of the Jamestown Baseball School and serves as assistant baseball coach for the Salve Regina University baseball team.

Coach Eric Cirella: The Reins Have Been Passed

We pick up Eric Cirella's story as a player at Salve Regina University—and what a story it is. Young Cirella made varsity his freshman year. He holds several Salve Regina University baseball career records, as well as two NCAA records for 2005. During his senior year (2005), he earned the NCAA batting crown with a .504 batting average and had the most walks, with forty-nine. Following is a list of some of his other achievements:

Eric Cirella's All-Time Career Offensive Records at Salve Regina University (2002–05)

Category	Rank	Stat
Batting Average	First	.447
Slugging Percentage	Tenth	.575
On-Base Percentage	First	.572
Games Played	Third	152
At-Bats	Fourth	492
Runs Scored	First	181
Hits	First	220
Doubles	First	49
Total Bases	Third	283
Walks	First	146
Stolen Bases	Third	87
Stolen Base Attempts	Third	93
Stolen Base Percentage	First	93% (87 out of 93)

Eric Cirella's All-Time Single-Season Offensive Records at Salve Regina University (2002–05)

Category	Rank	Stat	Year
Batting Average	Fourth	.514	2004
	Fifth	.504	2005
On-Base Percentage	First	.638	2005
	Second	.624	2004
Stolen Base Percentage	Second (tie)	1.000	2004
Games Played	Second (tie)	43	2005
Runs Scored	First	61	2004
	Second	58	2005
Hits	Third	65	2005
Doubles	First	21	2005
Walks	First	49	2005
	Third	42	2004
	Fourth	36	2003
Stolen Bases*	First	37	2005
	Second	34	2004
Stolen Base Attempts	First	40	2005
	Second (tie)	34	2004

*At one point, Cirella stole 50 straight bases without being caught.

Eric Cirella after College: Putting His Offensive Baseball Skills to Work

Immediately following college, Eric joined his father's coaching staff with the Seahawks, where he helped that team win thirty-two games. In 2006, Eric signed a professional contract with the Rockford River Hawks of the Frontier League but ended up with the New Haven County Cutters of the independent Canadian American Association that summer. He felt the situation wasn't right for him and left after getting into two games in right field, going one for four and scoring one run. This was the end of Eric's professional playing career.

Eric then signed on as assistant coach for the University of Rhode Island (URI), an extremely successful Division I college team. Over the next six seasons, Eric functioned in several capacities, including third-base coach specializing in base running, bunting, situational hitting and working with the outfielders. In his time with URI, the team amassed a record of 187 wins, 138 losses and 3 ties for a .576 winning percentage. URI also participated in the Atlantic 10 Conference tournament each year, finishing first one year, second in two years and no lower than fifth in the other years. (Historical note: The University of Rhode Island began in 1890 as a land-grant college in Kingston, Rhode Island. The school began to formally play baseball in 1898 and had a 6-2 record. In its long baseball history, URI has played in 2,547 games, winning 1,215. Since 2004, the team has averaged 34 wins a season, played in the Atlantic 10 tournament each year, held an NCAA regional berth and was named the top Division I baseball team in New England for the 2009 and 2012 seasons.)

In 2008, Eric signed on as a hitting instructor for the Green Bay Bullfrogs of the Northwoods League. There he helped the Bullfrogs lead the league in five offensive categories, including batting average, hits, doubles, triples and total bases. In 2012, Eric came back to help his father as assistant coach at Salve Regina University and, as noted earlier, took over as head coach for the 2014 season. For such a young individual, Eric has accomplished much.

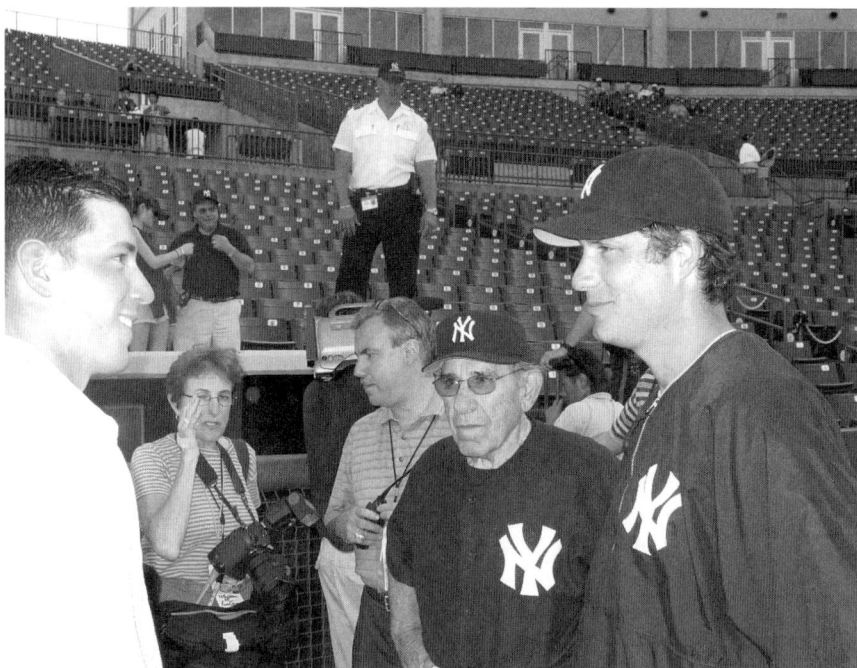

Damian Costantino (left) with Yogi Berra (center) and Robin Ventura (right), 2003. *Photo credit and courtesy Edward Habershaw.*

In his undergraduate college career, he was an all-conference and academic all-conference member for four years while also earning the 2004 Brother Michael Reynolds Award for outstanding accomplishment in academics and athletics. He was Salve Regina University's male athlete of the year in 2004–05 and a three-time Academic All-American in addition to earning the 2005 *ESPN The Magazine* Academic All-American of the Year Award. Following his 2004 and 2005 seasons, he was selected for the All-New England First Team and was a Rawlings ABCA All-American at shortstop and outfield. In 2005, he received the Vin Cullen Award for small college achievement by Words Unlimited.

Eric graduated magna cum laude from Salve Regina University with a BS in financial management. He was a member of the dean's list for four straight years. In 2010, Eric earned a master's degree in communication studies from the URI School of Communication. He also taught as a graduate instructor at URI from 2007 to 2009. In 2011, Eric became the youngest inductee into the Salve Regina Athletic Hall of Fame. It is evident that Eric Cirella will go on to accomplish great things in his coaching career, and the Salve University baseball program is in very good hands indeed.

ONE MORE SHORT STORY: DAMIAN COSTANTINO

It is my philosophy that every single human being on earth has stories worth telling; however, we all know it's not possible to tell all those stories in a single book. Consequently, I will highlight just one more individual connected to Salve Regina University baseball—Damian Costantino. Costantino had an excellent college baseball career, finishing in the top ten in the Salve Regina record books in many offensive categories. However, there is one statistic in which he stands alone. It is best stated in a story posted on SI.com in 2003.

PUTTING ON THE HITS
SALVE REGINA'S COSTANTINO BREAKS VENTURA'S
NCAA RECORD

Damian Costantino's name now represents for college baseball what Joe DiMaggio's means in the big leagues.
Costantino, who plays for Division III Salve Regina in Newport, R.I., broke New York Yankees third baseman Robin Ventura's NCAA record for

Damian Costantino during his record-breaking 2003 season. *Lehigh Photo*.

Steve Cirella (left), Robin Ventura (center) and Damian Costantino (right), 2003. *Photo credit and courtesy Edward Habershaw.*

consecutive games with a hit on Monday, singling against Mount Union (Ohio) to extend his run to 59.

Costantino, a 24-year-old junior outfielder from Warwick, R.I., hit an RBI single over the second base bag with one out in the third inning.

His teammates rushed the field to mob him as the play ended.

Starting on April Fools' Day 2001, Costantino began a long adventure into the annals of baseball history that did not end until two years and sixty games later. He accomplished something no other college player in the history of the NCAA had ever done before: sixty consecutive games with a hit!

It is time now time to end the Salve Regina University baseball story for the purposes of this book. However, Salve's story will certainly continue for many years into the future.

St. George's School Baseball

The Early Years: A Case Study of the Importance of Baseball in a Small Prestigious College-Prep School

St. George's School is a high-quality college-preparatory school serving 365 young men and women from Rhode Island, the rest of the United States and nineteen foreign countries. Currently located in Middletown, Rhode Island, the school sits on a hill overlooking beautiful First Beach in Newport. The location was described in a 1901 Newport Daily News article headlined "St. George's School: New Building Begun on a Commanding Site in Middletown."

The site certainly is commanding. When standing on the St. George's School grounds, you find yourself looking at a gorgeous panoramic view of the Atlantic Ocean. Looking up at St. George's School from Second Beach, you see a majestic Gothic-style structure that would do the mansions of Newport justice. But this was not always the case.

The school owes its humble beginnings to Reverend John Byron Diman, with financial backing from his mother and sister. Reverend Diman graduated from Brown University and earned a master's degree from Harvard. Records

St. George's School. *Courtesy St. George's School.*

do not indicate exactly why he began the school, but it was clear from the beginning that he was interested in running a well-disciplined, academically oriented school to emphasize classical learning, math and sciences. Although not athletically inclined himself, Reverend Diman utilized sports, especially baseball, to create a well-rounded student. Baseball was very important to both college-preparatory schools and the most prestigious institutions of higher learning in the late 1890s. A considerable amount of energy and school spirit on college campuses was dedicated to the baseball team. The admissions process for these colleges most likely scrutinized prospective students' participation in sports, especially baseball. At the time, football was in its infancy, and baseball was the dominant sport on college campuses. Experienced athletes were needed to feed the college baseball teams, particularly those of the Ivy League colleges and universities. A student from a college-prep school who had significant baseball involvement could very well have gained at least a small degree of favor during the application process. It is doubtful that Reverend Diman ignored the importance of preparing young men in this arena.

In 1896, Reverend Diman incorporated Diman's School for Boys through the Rhode Island General Assembly. (At that time, all corporations were created by acts of the Rhode Island General Assembly.) In the spring of 1896, he began running the following advertisement in the *Newport Mercury* and the *Newport Daily News*:

> *MR. JOHN B. DIMAN*
> *WILL OPEN A SMALL*
> *BOARDING SCHOOL FOR BOYS*
> *in Newport, October 1, 1896*
> *P.O. Box 154, Newport, RI*

The school was located in two leased adjacent cottages on Deblois Avenue (now Hunter Avenue). At its opening on October 1, the school had twelve students. Demonstrating the need to address both the physical "spirit" and the mental spirit, Reverend Diman wasted no time in securing a field where baseball could be played, as reported in the September 25, 1897 edition of the *Newport Daily News*: "O.D. Taylor has rented for this baseball association the baseball lot on Freebody Street to Mr. John H. [*sic*] Diman for the winter season. The grounds will be used by Mr. Diman's scholars for a playground." Note: Ball fields for school-age students during this time period were referred to as "playgrounds."

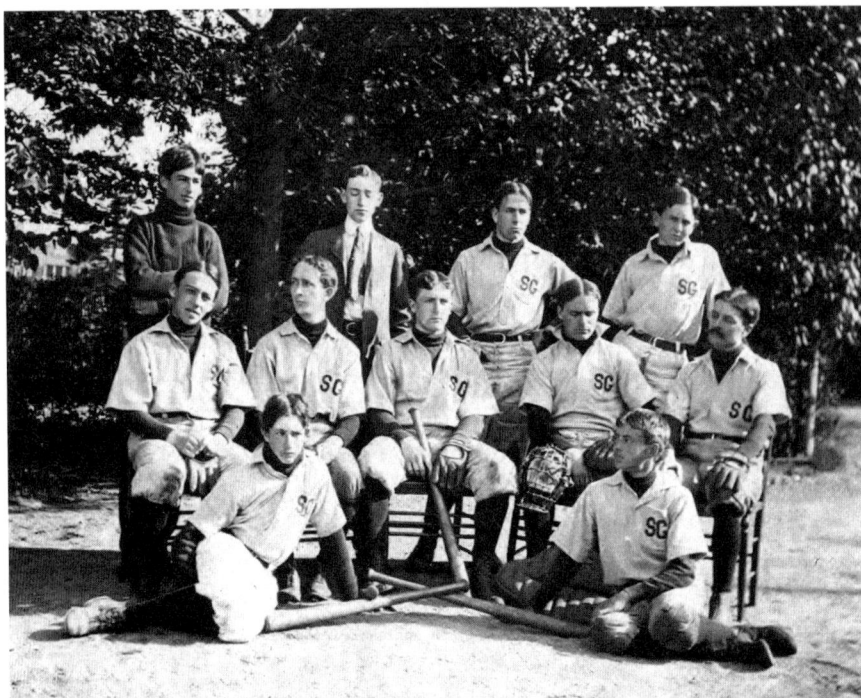

St. George's School baseball team, 1914. *Courtesy St. George's School.*

Opposite, top: St. George's School baseball team, circa 1900. *Courtesy St. George's School.*

Opposite, bottom: St. George's School baseball team, 1902. *Courtesy St. George's School.*

Throughout 1897 and 1898, baseball skills were being taught, and the school formed its first team in 1899. That year, the team played two games, both against Rogers High School. St. George's defeated Rogers High by the score of 20–7 in the first game, and the teams tied 24–24 in the second. These outcomes should be considered favorable since Rogers High School had been playing for many years.

Four Special Alumni Baseball Players

All of the following individuals are notable, and each has an interesting story. However, to tell a story adequately and to tie it to the themes of this book, we will restrict our examination to four famous St. George's alumni who played on the school's baseball team. Two of them played on the 1910 team: Philip Drinker and Prescott Sheldon Bush.

St. George's School baseball team, 1910. Prescott Sheldon Bush, father of President George H.W. Bush and grandfather of President George W. Bush, can be seen in the bottom row, third from left. Philip Drinker, inventor of the iron lung, is in the second row, second from left. *Courtesy St. George's School.*

Philip Drinker

Philip Drinker was born on December 12, 1894, in Haverford, Pennsylvania, and died in Fritzwilliam, New Hampshire, on October 19, 1972. His father was a railroad man and the president of Lehigh University. Drinker, who graduated from St. George's in 1911, was not a starter on the baseball team, and we do not know what position he played. We do know that his professional work resulted in saving thousands of future lives. After graduating from St. George's, he attended Princeton University, graduating in 1915. He took a position teaching at the Harvard Medical School and, later, the Harvard School of Public Health. Drinker was well known for his textbooks and scholarly works on a variety of topics in industrial hygiene. In 1929, he invented the Drinker Respirator, which later became known as the iron lung. The iron lung saved countless lives of people who contracted polio, were victims of coal gas poisoning or suffered from other serious respiratory diseases. Philip Drinker retired from Harvard in the early 1960s and was inducted into the United States National Inventors Hall of Fame in 2007.

America's Pastime in the City by the Sea

Prescott Sheldon Bush

Prescott Sheldon Bush was born on May 15, 1895, in Columbus, Ohio, and died on October 8, 1972. Bush played on the baseball team from 1910 through 1913, when he graduated. He was an athletic young man and played first base for the St. George's team, serving as captain of the 1911, 1912 and 1913 teams. These teams were some of best fielded by St. George's, winning 31 games against 17 losses. Only the 1912 team had a losing record. The 1911 team went 10-3, and the 1913 team boasted an 11-5 record. Bush graduated from Yale, where he was a cheerleader, president of the Yale Glee Club and played varsity golf, football and baseball. During World War I, he was a captain of field artillery with the American Expeditionary Forces from 1917 through 1919. He also served as an intelligence officer, assisting the French Army.

After the war, Bush engaged in a business career, working in management and owning several very successful businesses. He was the treasurer for the first national campaign of Planned Parenthood in 1947 and was an early supporter of the United Negro College Fund. As a freshman U.S. senator from Connecticut, Bush took a strong stand against Senator Joseph McCarthy in the 1950s, stating that the Wisconsin senator's Communist-hunting tactics had "caused dangerous divisions among American people because of his attitude and the attitude he has encouraged among his followers: that there can be no honest differences of opinion with him. Either you must follow Senator McCarthy blindly, not daring to express any doubts or disagreements about any of his actions, or, in his eyes, you must be a Communist, a Communist sympathizer, or a fool who has been duped by the Communist line." Bush served in the Senate from 1952 to 1963. He was the father of President George H.W. Bush and the grandfather of President George W. Bush and former Florida governor Jeb Bush.

Ogden Nash

Ogden Nash was born on August 19, 1902, in Rye, New York, and died on May 19, 1971, in Baltimore, Maryland. Nash played on the St. George's baseball team, although not as a starter. After graduating in 1920, he entered Harvard University but dropped out a year later. He returned to St. George's School to teach for a year before moving to New York City. He worked in sales before taking a job writing streetcar ads for the same company that employed another future well-known writer, F. Scott Fitzgerald. Nash also wrote for the *New Yorker* magazine and went on to become one of America's most famous poets. He once stated that since he was a child, he loved to rhyme. He wrote a poem for

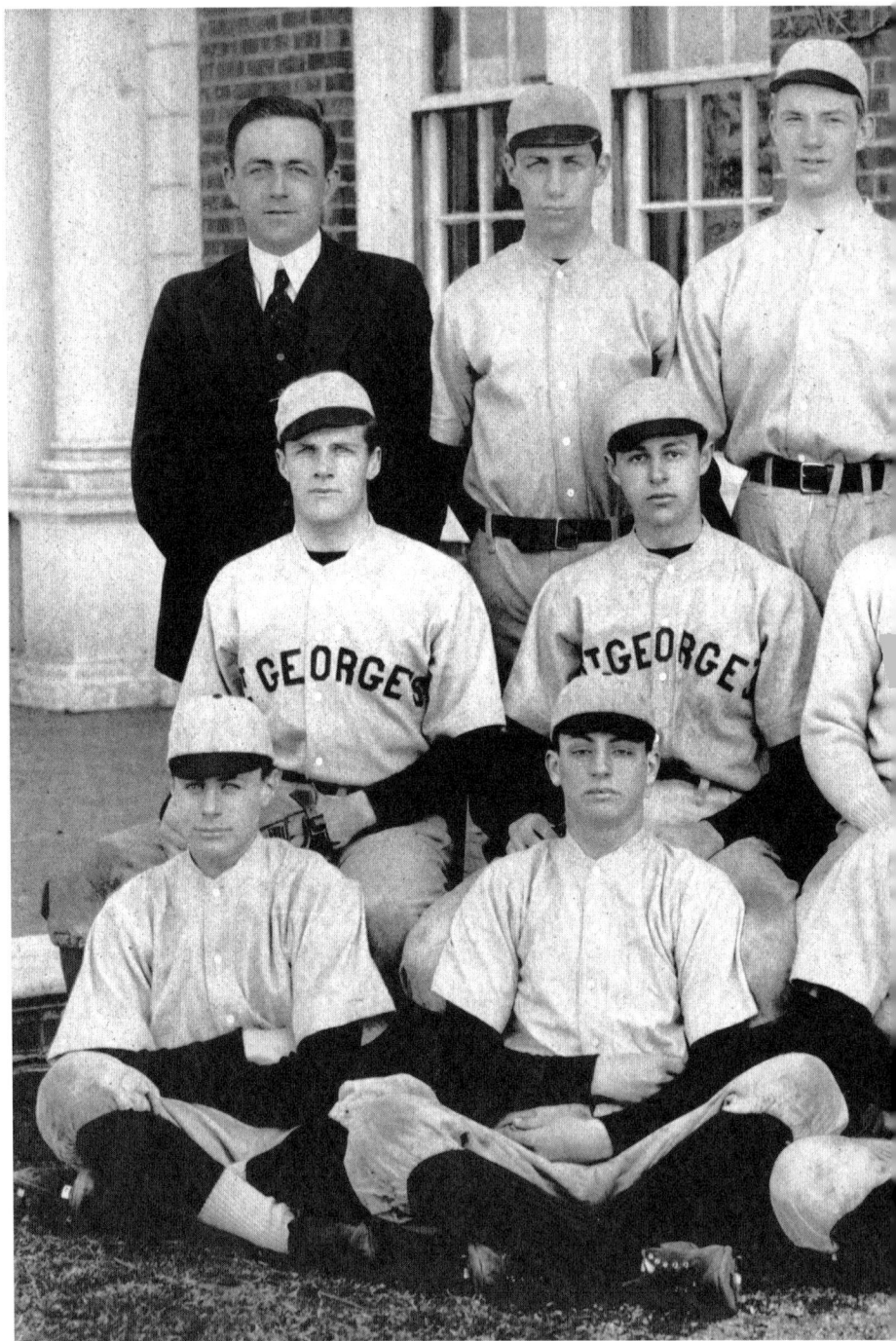

St. George's School baseball team, 1920. Ogden Nash is pictured in the bottom row, third from left. *Courtesy St. George's School.*

the January 1949 issue of *Sport* magazine entitled "Line-Up for Yesterday: An ABC of Baseball Immortals." The poem, which used twenty-four letters of the alphabet to represent players' names, honored baseball greats such as Grover Cleveland Alexander (A), Ty Cobb (T), Dizzy Dean (D), Lou Gehrig and many others. Following is the verse for "I":

> *I is for Me*
> *Not a hard-hitting man,*
> *But an outstanding all-time*
> *Incurable fan.*

Geza P. Teleki

Geza Teleki was born in Hungary on December 7, 1943. He attended St. George's from 1958 to 1962 and played varsity baseball. After graduating from St. George's, Teleki obtained a baccalaureate degree from George Washington University and earned a master's degree in anthropology from Pennsylvania State University in 1970. He eventually earned his doctorate in physical anthropology from the University of Georgia in 1977.

Teleki spent two years as a graduate student living with wild chimpanzees under the tutelage of Jane Goodall at the Gombe Stream Game Reserve in Tanganyika. He was a tenacious advocate for animal rights and authored many papers related to primates, including "They Are Us," as well as worked on several projects that helped children understand primates in our world.

Teleki's father and grandfather are notable individuals in Hungarian history. His father, also named Geza, was a professor chairing the Geology Department at George Washington University and also once served as the minister of education in Hungary. His grandfather, Count Paul Teleki, twice served as prime minister of Hungary and was a world-renowned geographer.

Later in life, Teleki would become heavily involved as a volunteer member of the community panel in the Spring Valley neighborhood of Washington, D.C. The panel was formed to oversee the cleanup of an old U.S. Army Chemical Corps dumping ground for munitions and chemical warfare products. According to a November 29, 2012 article in the *Washington Post*, the neighborhood contained "more than 500 items related to munitions, such as bottles of arsenic trichloride and canister shells of liquid mustard, have been removed from the residential property on Glenbrook Road during two investigations between 2000 and 2010. The Army has also removed 400 pounds of laboratory glass and 100 tons of contaminated soil in that time. The Army has been removing buried munitions there since 1993."

A "MASTER" IN SCIENCE AND BASEBALL: WILLIAM PIKE ELLIOTT

(Author's note: For the piece on William Pike Elliott, I primarily utilized an unpublished paper, "Experience Excellence: The Story of William Pike Elliott and St. George's School," written by John G. Doll, class of 1952 and school archivist, written on May 21, 2005.)

St. George's made a good hire in the fall of 1927 when it engaged the services of a very young William Pike Elliott. A new graduate out of Dartmouth College, he was hired as the "master" for science. He was also named head coach of the football team. Born in 1905 in Newburyport, Massachusetts, Elliott concentrated on his studies throughout his youth. However, he also concentrated on another activity: baseball. An outstanding high school athlete, he was recruited to play baseball and football at the college level. However, perhaps he was not keenly aware of the names of those colleges, as relayed by Mr. Doll in his article: "A (perhaps apocryphal) story has made the rounds that when he was asked by the Dartmouth recruiter if he'd like to play ball for Dartmouth, a young Mr. Elliott responded, 'What's Dartmouth?'"

Of course, Mr. Elliott was known to have a wry sense of humor. He got used to the idea of Dartmouth and went on to have an outstanding baseball career, even serving as captain during his senior year. In 1931, after four years at St. George's, he finally was named head coach of the baseball team. Here he excelled in coaching the young men in baseball and life. Elliott remained head baseball coach until leaving the school in 1952. One of his best baseball years was 1935, when his team went 8-2 and beat longtime rival Middlesex. The rivalry between Middlesex and St. George's could be considered one of historical proportions. The athletic contests between the two schools were so important that each school's yearbook published an updated record of the football and baseball games. Middlesex had a decidedly favorable outcome in regards to baseball. In 1935, when Elliott's team beat Middlesex, there was jubilation on the school campus, as demonstrated in the June 5, 1935 edition of the school paper, *The Red & White*:

After the victories at Middlesex Saturday, the School rejoiced with all the bells, sirens, and horns they could get a hold of. Mr. Roberts, in a Schoolroom meeting, called off evening study hall and told the boys they could build a bonfire below North Field. He added that Mr. Christie had purchased some fireworks for the school to celebrate with. Soon everyone was in old clothes and the wood was piled up for the fire. Some of the Third

Formers made an effigy which they christened "The Jinx" and hung at the summit of the pyre.

Coaching is an art form. One can be a bad coach, a mediocre coach, an excellent coach or fall within the gradations between. Being an excellent coach requires dedication, skills, a great disposition and effective communication. By all accounts, Elliott appears to have been a coach of the highest order and an important fixture at St. George's for all the students who went there, especially the baseball players. He was equally appreciated for his work on the football team and for his teaching capabilities. Upon his departure, he was eulogized in the April 16, 1952 edition of *The Red & White*:

> *The school learns with the deepest regret of Mr. Elliott's decision to leave in June. His 25 years of service to St. George's have left behind a record of devotion, unselfishness, and genuine interests which have endeared him to Masters and boys alike. Whether on the athletic field, in the classroom, or in the "office," his ready wit and capable understanding of problems have made him "tops" in the eyes of everyone in the school family. He and "Mrs. E" have secured themselves in the affections of countless boys over the years through their unceasingly friendly hospitality in their home. It is therefore on the behalf of many, that the "Red & White" wishes them the best of luck and gratefully acknowledges the contributions which have earned for them so deservedly our wholehearted praise for a job well done.*

William Pike Elliott passed away on August 10, 1993, at the age of eighty-seven. Perhaps his life's philosophy, which he passed on to the young men he coached, can be best demonstrated by a quote from the November 5, 1944 edition of *The Red & White*: "Everyone should have the opportunity to experience excellence…to let them know that there is something constructive each one of them can and will do even in this confused culture of today."

REMINISCING: THE FIRST FIVE DECADES OF BASEBALL AT ST. GEORGE'S SCHOOL

Baseball has been played at St. George's for more than a century. Following is a brief summary of the first five decades. The team played a very limited schedule through 1902. In 1903, a full schedule of baseball was up and running, with 11 games played. In 1917, the team played eight games, with the remainder being canceled due to concerns relating to World War I. The school's baseball teams played a total of 501 games from 1899 through 1951. Not counting the missing games and years from the records that are available, we can determine that St. George's teams amassed 220 wins, 274 losses and 7 ties. In terms of wins, the best seasons came in these years:

1903: 8-2-1
1904: 9-1
1911: 10-3
1913: 11-5
1922: 8-2
1927: 7-1
1935: 8-2
1941: 8-1
1944: 7-2
1950: 7-1-2
1951: 10-0

The 1951 campaign was the only undefeated season. It is interesting to note that it was common practice at college-preparatory schools for the masters (teachers) of the school to play alongside the students during games.

A little horseplay at St. George's School, 1914. *Courtesy St. George's School.*

Keeping score at St. George's School, circa 1910. *Courtesy St. George's School.*

In the early 1900s, Reverend Diman found it necessary to stop this practice because the masters were taking the games too seriously and, according to his reminiscences, tended to take over the game.

STILL AN IMPORTANT SPORT

St. George's School played over sixty years of baseball beyond what is covered in this narrative. Baseball remains a very important sport at the school, teaching discipline, teamwork, good sportsmanship and adjustment to the highs and lows of life. It also contributes to the school spirit. Today, players have a beautiful ball field on which to play, and St. George's continues to engage area high school teams. There is no doubt that as long as the old stone relief of a baseball player on the old North Slype Door remains overlooking the school grounds, the grand old game will be alive and well at St. George's School.

THE GULLS OF NEWPORT

Newport must be one of those mystical vortexes where the metaphysical properties of the universe converge to create magic—not illusions but the real thing. It's a place where baseball happens in an unusual way. As I have tumbled over the years into the space-time continuum we call research, one thing becomes evident: there is a consistency beyond expectation proving this is a special place where teams are born to play high-quality and winning baseball—not just in terms of winning percentage but also in terms of a win for the community and its people. Every baseball team story told or referenced in this book—and many that are not mentioned—literally carries with it the effervescence of specialness. The Gulls are no different.

Before coming to Newport, the Gulls' predecessors, the Rhode Island Reds and Rhode Island Gulls, certainly had a few winning seasons, But they never won a championship. The team became the Newport Gulls in 2001, and the record speaks for itself.

Year	Wins	Losses	Winning Percentage
2001*	25	15	.625
2002*	25	17	.595
2003	25	15	.625
2004	26	15	.634
2005*	25	16	.605
2006	32	10	.761
2007	25	17	.595
2008	26	16	.619
2009*	31	10	.756
2010	27	15	.658
2011	29	13	.690
2012*	31	10	.756
2013	30	14	.682
Total	357	183	.661

* = championship year

The Gulls have accomplished 357 total wins in thirteen summers for an average of 27.5 wins per season and an overall winning percentage of .661. Unbelievable! When you consider the fact that they have earned five championships and have never had a season with a winning percentage below .595, it is not hard to see how this team came to be highlighted in this book. The extraordinary aura that surrounds the Gulls does not stop with their won/loss record. The Gulls have also had a total of 162 players ascend to the professional ranks, five of whom are in the major leagues: Jeff Beliveau (Chicago Cubs), Mitchell Boggs (St. Louis Cardinals), Chris Iannetta (Los Angeles Angels), Jason Szuminski (San Diego Padres) and Adam Wilk (Detroit Tigers).

If I were a young ballplayer, I certainly would strongly consider playing for the Newport Gulls. They play in a great city and have a great winning tradition, a great coaching staff, a great ball field (Cardines) and, lest we forget, a great public address announcer—Don O'Hanley. A little more about him later.

The Newport Gulls play in a fine example of an amateur collegiate baseball league. The New England Collegiate Baseball League (NECBL) was founded in 1993 under the leadership of Emmy Award–winning television producer/director Joseph Consentino, who, among other things, had played minor-league outfield for the Red Sox. The first commissioner was the great George Foster, former All Star player for the Cincinnati Reds and New York Mets. Play began in 1994, and the league has developed into one of the nation's top-tier amateur leagues, with representation from all six New England states. Rhode Island entered in 1996 with the Rhode Island Reds, who played in Cranston. In 1999, a second team, the Rhode Island Gulls, joined and played in West Warwick. The league now sports thirteen teams in two divisions and has become one of the most successful leagues in the country.

Now back to Gull's Hall of Famer Don O'Hanley. Mr. O'Hanley is much more than the team's public address announcer. He is a longtime baseball historian and researcher and has contributed significantly in these areas. He takes pride in adding historical anecdotes and getting the players names pronounced correctly. In a recent press article, he perfectly describes his philosophy of announcing: "My idea is to treat the microphone in a conversational fashion. Be easygoing, and you'll keep your audience interested; they won't will feel like they're being lectured to."

Don O'Hanley is a fellow Society for American Baseball Research (SABR) member and a constant contributor to the overall knowledge of baseball history. At age eighty, he certainly has a few decades of direct observation and experience from which to work. He definitely will be this baseball researcher/author's mentor for many years to come.

Chapter 5

BALL FIELDS

FROM THE BASIN TO CARDINES FIELD: THE EVOLUTION OF THE MOST BEAUTIFUL BALL FIELD IN RHODE ISLAND

The following was published in the September 9, 1891 issue of the *Newport Mercury*: "The work affiliated with filling the basin near the Old Colony depot is being prosecuted with good results. About 200 carloads of dirt have been dumped each day during the past week. It is thought that about four months will be required to complete the work."

The land area known as the Basin (ball field) was born in 1891. The original water-filled basin from which the area got its name was a reservoir surrounded by stone walls and fed by several springs. Once filled in, this land was destined to become home to one of the most beautiful ballparks in the country, Cardines Field, and the extremely popular tourist destination called the Brick Market. The first ballgame known to have been played on the Basin was recorded in the following humorous article published in the July 31, 1899 issue of the *Newport Daily News*. (It should be noted that some historians have made reference to ball being played as early as 1893 on the Basin; however, I have not been able to verify that year.)

There was a ballgame Saturday afternoon on the Basin lot, between the Real Things and the Has Beens, of the Old Colony Repair Shop. The

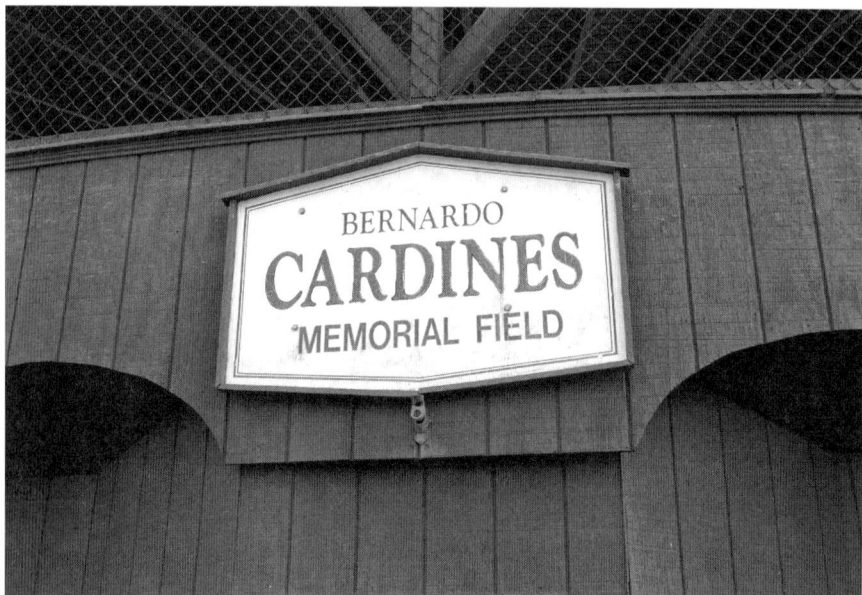

Bernardo Cardines Memorial Field edifice, 2013. *Photo credit author.*

Cardines Field, 2013. *Photo credit author.*

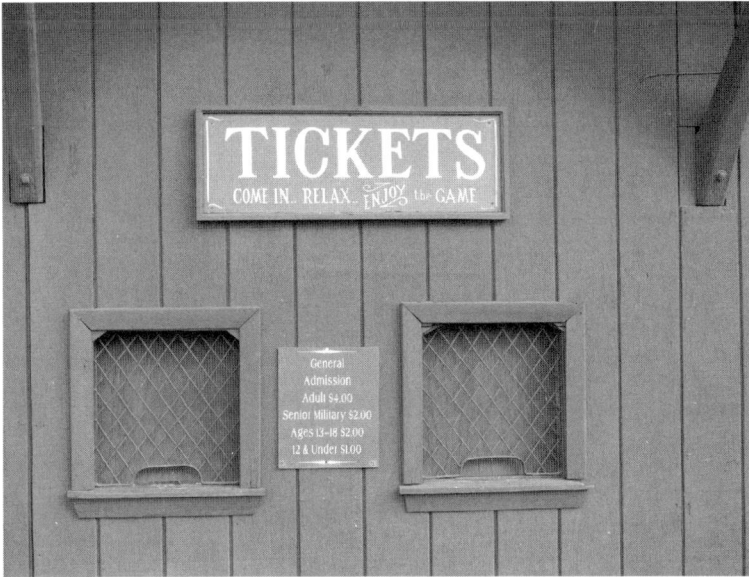

Above: Ticket windows at Cardines Field, 2013. *Author's collection.*

Right: A shot of the outside overhead at Cardines Field, 2013. *Photo credit author.*

contest was to decide which should carry the name of the Old Colony Base Ball Club. The Has Beens showed their superiority, or perhaps they had better luck; at any rate, when 9 innings had been played without the police being called and/or the umpire mobbed, it was found that the Has Beens had 14 runs to their credit, while the Real Things had the unlucky number of 13. Now the Has Beens are the Real Things and the Real Things are nothing, so far as the Old Colony name is concerned. There probably will be another contest later. The batteries were Egan, Sullivan and Hackett for the victors and Gill and Cleary for the victims.

Despite the Basin having been filled in, the land remained mushy and often contained surface water that tended to stink, much to the displeasure of the neighbors. In 1908, the installation of sewer drains cleared off considerable amounts of the water and made it possible for the area to be used as a field for children's running and jumping events and for the occasional carnival. In 1908, according to an old undated and unidentified news clipping owned by George Donnelly Jr., a group of men working at the Old Colony Repair Shop obtained permission from the New York, New Haven and Hartford Railroad Company to use the field for baseball games. The field was dangerous because of the many holes, broken bottles, tin cans and stones, as well as its electrical poles and wires. Men from the Old Colony's Boiler Makers volunteered many hours after work to bring the field into shape so that baseball could be played at the site.

The first serious baseball played on the Basin was brought about by the formation of the City Base Ball League in 1908. Under the auspices of this league, the first game was played on the remodeled field on May 25, 1908. In the first year of the league, there were six teams: the Torpedo Station Clerks, the Rudder Club, the Rangers, the Old Colony team, the Primer Makers and the YMCA team. The race was close down to the wire, and the Torpedo Station Clerks won the championship, with the Old Colony team finishing second. It is also believed that the forerunner of the soon-to-be famous semipro Trojans played a game or two on the Basin in 1908.

In its inaugural year, the Basin's average attendance was about seven hundred. There were no bleachers or seats of any kind, and spectators could be seen lining the outfield and sidewalks. The park was not without some amenities, however—it did have benches for the players. An old discarded fishnet thrown over the backstop sufficed to keep foul balls from going over

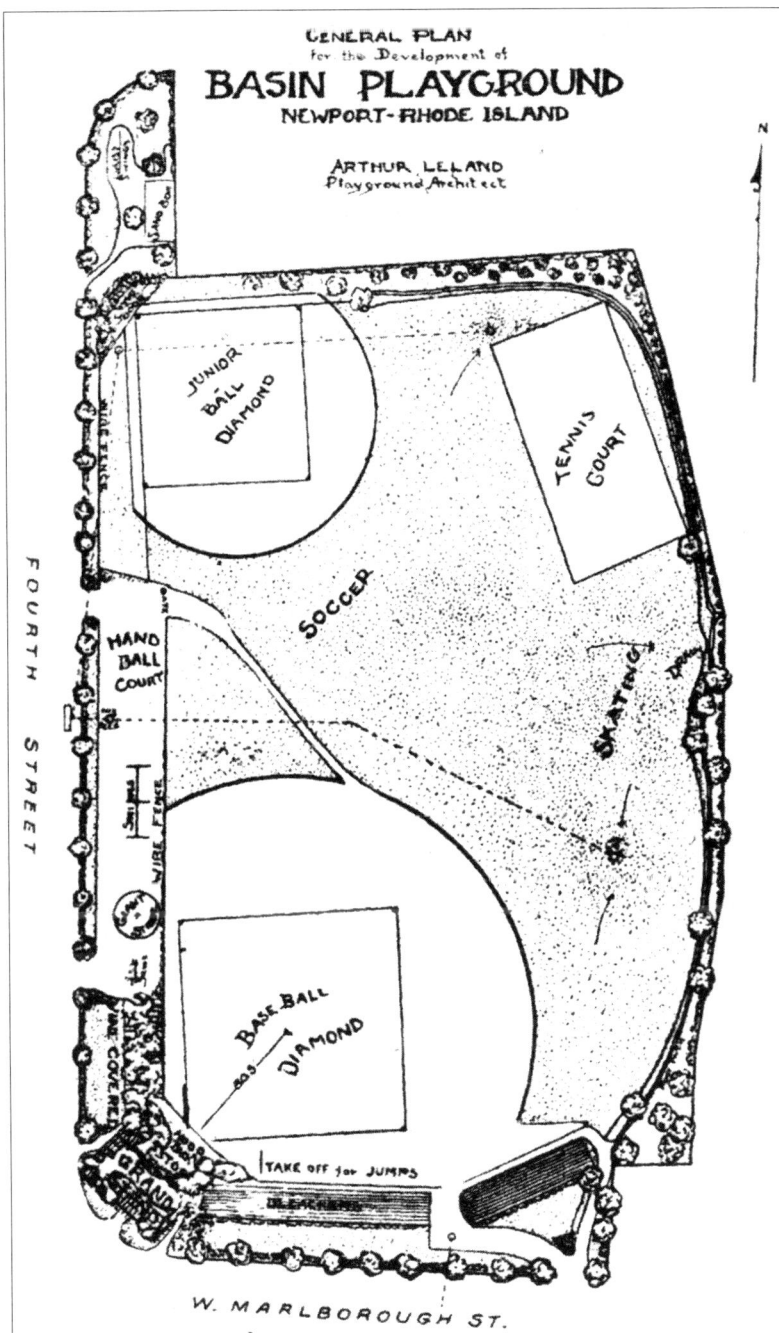

GENERAL PLAN
for the Development of
BASIN PLAYGROUND
NEWPORT - RHODE ISLAND

ARTHUR LELAND
Playground Architect

N

JUNIOR BALL DIAMOND

TENNIS COURT

SOCCER

HAND BALL COURT

SKATING

FOURTH STREET

BASE BALL DIAMOND

TAKE OFF for JUMPS

W. MARLBOROUGH ST.

Arthur Leland's proposed layout for Cardines Field in the 1920s included a handball court, two baseball diamonds, a tennis court and soccer grounds. *Courtesy George Donnelly Jr.*

Downtown Newport after the Great Hurricane of 1938. *Author's collection.*

to the railroad station and disturbing the horses and carriages awaiting arrival of the passenger trains. However, there was one problem that caused considerable angst for railroad officials. With no high fences, it was not uncommon for foul balls to break the windows of passing trains. There is no record of how this irritation was resolved.

Continued small improvements were made through 1919, when the original Sunset League began using the field along with Wellington Avenue and Freebody Park. In 1936, the City of Newport took ownership of the park. Records from 1936–37 show that the Works Progress Administration (WPA) built stone and concrete bleachers on the third-base side. After the devastating hurricane of 1938, the WPA built the grandstand, and in 1939, the signature curved part of the grandstand behind home plate was constructed. Over the years, other construction projects increased capacity. The park was designed in a way to mimic many of the old-time ballparks such as Fenway Park, Ebbets Field and Wrigley Field. (A number of major-league and professional players played at this park during World War II, including Yogi Berra, Phil Rizzuto and Bob Feller.)

The Basin was renamed the Bernardo Cardines Memorial Field in 1936, as reported in the August 28, 1936 edition of the *Newport Mercury and Weekly News*.

VFW TO DEDICATE NEW MEMORIAL FIELD
Basin to be Called Bernardo Cardines Memorial Field
Mayor and Other Prominent Speakers Will Partake in
Exercises Sunday Afternoon

The basin playground, which has been extensively renovated, will be dedicated as the Bernardo Cardines Memorial Field Sunday, September 20, by the Veterans of Foreign Wars. Formal exercises will mark the occasion, with Veterans being assisted by a number of local Italian clubs. C.J. Juckowski, post commander of the veterans post, heads the arrangements committee.

This dedication is in accordance with the plans of the Veterans of Foreign Wars, which has named other playfields, squares, and parks throughout the city in honor of those killed in action during the World War. Those co-operating include the Italian Brothers, Sons of Italy, the Italo-American Club, and the Italo Republican and Italo Democratic clubs of the country.

(Historical note: Private Bernardo Cardines, Company M, 310th Infantry, was the first Newport native to be killed in action in World War I. He died in the Battle of Saint-Mihiel, which was fought from September 12–15,

Mudville Pub, 2013. *Photo credit author.*

1918. It was the first battle totally directed by General John J. Pershing, commander of the American Expeditionary Force (AEF). In addition to the AEF, General Pershing also had forty-eight thousand French troops under his command. This was one of the first battles in which the U.S. Army Air Service played an important role. Due to the unexpected success of this battle, the American forces gained a great amount of respect from the French and British soldiers.)

After the renovations in 1938, the park was used by many teams and city leagues, most notably the George Donnelly Sunset League. The park remains one of the most used parks in Newport to this day. Besides the Sunset League, it is also used by the Gulls of the well-known New England Collegiate Baseball League.

On a nice summer evening, if you are lucky, you can enjoy a couple brewskis or sodas while sitting on the back deck of the Mudville Pub on West Marlborough Street. From this vantage point, you are practically on top of right field. Then again, if one is not of the persuasion to take in some "spirits," the grandstand seats are perfectly situated, and there's not a bad one in the house.

FREEBODY PARK, WELLINGTON GROUNDS AND OTHER BALLPARKS OF NEWPORT
Freebody Park

Freebody Park lies on a large tract of land on Freebody Street. The land was originally donated to the city in the 1870s. City planners initially had some difficulty deciding what to do with the plot. The following short mention of the property appeared in the May 7, 1873 edition of the *Newport Daily News*:

> *The report of the commissioners on the Freebody land was received. The report states that the work on the land has been done satisfactorily, and recommends a commissioner be appointed to see that the land is properly leased. It is suggested that there be a new appraisal every seven years and that the rental be [illegible] percent on its last value, with exemption from city taxes.*

Discussion about the Freebody land appears to disappear from the public eye until a short mention in the March 17, 1881 edition of the *Newport Daily News*:

The Casino, circa 1900. *Author's collection.*

The suggestion that the Freebody land, so much of it as may be needed, be taken as a site for a new asylum for the poor meets with such favor. It was given for the benefit of the poor and this will be a practical method for carrying out the donor's wish.

Whether an asylum was built is not known. However, on June 21, 1882, the following article appeared in the *Newport Daily News*:

Petitions of J.F. Flynn, Jr., George Stevens and others, asking that a portion of the Freebody land, about 300 x 400 feet, be set apart as a Base Ball ground for the use of ball players, who have no place where they can play without trespassing or annoying residents, was referred to the governors of the poor.

By July 1882, baseball was being played regularly on the grounds, and it has been played there ever since. Most of Newport's leagues and teams have used the park throughout the years, and it has been constantly upgraded. Other events have been held there, too. Freebody Park was home to the Newport Jazz Festival from 1962 through 1964. It also hosted the Newport

Folk Festival in the mid-'60s, which included appearances by Bob Dylan, Joan Baez and others. The park has also been referred to as the Berkeley Grounds in 1889, as well as the Middletown Avenue grounds. It might also have been referred to as Gammell Park in 1897.

Wellington Park

Wellington Park was built in 1908 specifically for the Newport Ponies of the ill-fated Atlantic Association. Although many military and other teams played at Wellington Park, the primary user and owner of the lease was the great Trojans ballclub, which played there from 1909 to 1920, with the exception of when the park was leased to the U.S. Navy in 1918. In 1920, the wooden bleachers were removed and sold. The last written mention of the park being used was in 1938.

Kings Park

Kings Park is a relatively new park and is located off Wellington Avenue.

Coasters Island Park

Coasters Island Park has seen numerous names and locations on Coasters Island. The first written record of a baseball game being played on the

The U.S. Navy training station at Coasters Island, 1920. *Author's collection.*

island dates to 1875. The island has also been home to the Torpedo Station Training Grounds, the Naval Training Grounds, Farragut Field, the Second District Navy Grounds (both practice field and playing field) and the Coasters Harbor Island Grounds. A nice field currently exists on the island, and there is also an old dilapidated field, abandoned many years ago.

Vernon Avenue Grounds

The Vernon Avenue Grounds have been in existence since about 1913, and a ball field is still in existence. The field was also known at times as Cottrell Field.

Richmond Field

Richmond Field, located near the Wellington Avenue grounds, is named after the Richmond Manufacturing Company. The earliest recorded use of this field was in 1923, and the latest was in 1926. The Richmonds, a good semiprofessional team, were the main users of the field and played with an excellent stable of talent.

Coddington Park

This park, still in use, first appeared in news reports in about 1918.

Old Polo Grounds

The Old Polo Grounds were located on one of the corners of Narragansett Avenue and Thames Street. The area was first used for baseball in 1874 and as late as 1905.

The Broadway Lot

The Broadway Lot, circa 1912, was most likely located on Broadway.

Fort Adams Grounds

The Fort Adams Grounds were first used in 1874. They continued to be used as baseball grounds at least through the 1930s. Today, the modern-day Providence Grays still play games there, although there is no longer a diamond in the common area.

Morton Park

Morton Park was also known as the Vaughan Pond Grounds. The first baseball game can be traced to 1876. The park is still in existence, although there is no longer a baseball diamond there.

Murphy Field

Murphy Field begins to show up in the reports in 1923 and continues to be mentioned through 1936. The park still exists, but there is no ball field. This could be the same location as Richmond Field.

Gladding Lot

Gladding Lot was in use in 1905.

Malbone Road

The Malbone Road lot was in use in 1905.

Southwick's Grove

The location of Southwick's Grove remains a mystery despite many attempts to locate the Grove and inquiries with local historians. The Grove hosted baseball games from 1889 to 1892.

Chapter 6

TWO SPECIAL PLAYERS

FRANK CORRIDON: ALLEGED INVENTOR OF THE SPITBALL

Corridon's Baseball Beginnings

Frank Corridon honed his baseball skills while playing for Rogers High School in Newport in the mid-1890s. As a senior, his pitching drew the attention of Newport Colts manager Mike Finn, who signed Corridon for the 1899 season. (The Colts played in the Class-B New England League.) However, deterred by Corridon's lack of maturity, Finn released him early in the season. Corridon was quickly signed by the Pawtucket Colts of the same league. (Author's note: Both Pawtucket and Newport called themselves the Colts in 1899, which most likely caused some confusion.) Following is the story of Corridon's release, as reported in the *Newport Daily News* on June 26, 1899:

CORRIDON'S RELEASE

The Pawtucket Times *made merry over Manager Finn's letting Corridon go, after their last victory over Manchester.* [Author's note: Corridon was showing great success with the Colts and got the win over Manchester.] *Among the things it said was the following: "It would be interesting to get a line on Manager Finn's thoughts these beautiful days."*

A circa 1910 Polar Bear Cigarette Co. trading card for Frank Corridon. *Author's collection.*

Now, it is not known just what Mr. Finn thinks, and he does say that he left Corridon behind on the trip down East because both Gannon and Smith were to report, and it was a needless expense to have five pitchers. He also says he had a talk with Corridon the other day, and then he said that the stories going around about the differences between Corridon and the Newport team do not come from him: that he is on the best of terms with Manager Finn and all the members of the team, and that he feels they could not have done more to support him when he pitched. Manager Finn further says he knows the release of Corridon was an unpopular one, as the boy had many friends in the city. Still, everyone is liable to mistakes, and in this matter of holding or releasing players…he thinks Newport has made very few mistakes.

Finn feels that, while Corridon has the making of a good player in him, and promises well, he needs more experience to hold his own in the league, and Newport being in the rear at the seating could not well afford to try young pitchers when it could get old, experienced ones…He thinks the release was really a good thing for the boy, as the lad made a good impression by his work on the local teams, and thinks he will get a chance with the Pawtucket team, where he will really have a better opportunity to show his real ability than in his native city (Newport).

Later that summer, Corridon had the pleasure of returning to Newport and, with loud cheers from the locals, defeating the Colts. He went on to pitch 182 innings for the Pawtucket Colts in 1899.

More on Corridon's Professional Career

Following is the scouting report on Frank Corridon by J. Ed Grillo:

To Jack Ryder,

Corridon is a great pitcher, intelligent and willing. [He] has always been a winner in the spring and fall, and if worked with good judgment during the hot spell can deliver then. He is not a man of robust physique, and should not be used too often. I know of two American League clubs who would jump at a chance to get him. I should judge that he is a pitcher whom Griffith would make a better use than any one else because he is of the Griffith style of pitchers. He has always pitched his best against the best teams. He has excellent habits. Consider him Ewing's superior.

J. Ed Grillo,
Washington, January 18

In 1900, Corridon signed with the Eastern (International) League Providence Clamdiggers, known as the Providence Grays in most years of their existence. That same year, he was farmed out to Norwich of the Connecticut League, where he won fifteen games and lost only three. By 1901, he was playing full time with the Clamdiggers, pitching in thirty-five games and winning seventeen. In 1902, Corridon had perhaps his best professional year, leading the Eastern League with twenty-eight wins.

In 1904, Corridon was purchased by the Chicago Cubs and later traded to the Philadelphia A's. He played in the majors for six years between 1903 and 1910, finishing his major-league career with the St. Louis Cardinals. Despite the impression given by Grillo's scouting report, Corridon was not frail. In fact, he averaged 230 innings pitched per year in the majors and was extremely durable. Over his six-year major-league career, his ERA was 3.02. His best major-league season was with the Athletics in 1908, when he won 18 games, pitched 274 innings and sported a 2.46 ERA. Corridon followed this performance in 1909 with an 11-7 record (.611) and a 2.11 ERA. In his six seasons in the majors, he compiled a 70-67 record, 7 saves and a 2.80 ERA. In today's market, that would earn him a multimillion-dollar contract and would undoubtedly result in more wins.

In 1911, Corridon moved on to Buffalo of the Eastern League. As a player/manager in Buffalo, he compiled an 11-8 record while appearing in 32 games. The Buffalo Bisons ended the season at 74-75. In 1913, Corridon managed the Springfield Ponies of the Eastern Association to a 60-70 record. Corridon retired from professional baseball at the end of the '13 season and opened a small store on the corner of Russell Avenue and Malbone Road in Newport. However, he wasn't quite finished with baseball.

After the Pros

In 1914, Corridon organized and played for the Newport North Ends, a semipro team. When the United States entered World War I, he coached the navy's Second District team, stationed at the submarine station in Newport. The Second District team had some excellent players, including Rhode Islander John Gilmore. According to Gilmore's grandson, the Second District team was founded by former president Theodore Roosevelt, who frequented home games in Newport at the old Wellington Avenue ball grounds. (Roosevelt summered in Newport in 1917 and 1918.) The team was so good that when the navy could support only one team in the Northeast, it chose the Newport team over Boston's First District team. Roosevelt was responsible for the development of the Second District team, which he hoped would improve public relations between local residents and the booming population of navy personnel caused by the war. The assignment of local hero Frank Corridon to coach the team was no accident. Everyone loved Corridon, and as evidenced by local news coverage of the team, navy relations with the locals definitely improved.

After the war, Corridon returned to his roots, coaching the Rogers High team for several years. No matter where his baseball travels took him, Corridon always returned. Although he died in Syracuse, his body was returned to Newport for burial. Not only is Corridon held in high esteem nationally and locally for his contributions and accomplishments in baseball, but he remains the only Newport native son to play in the major leagues. Newport honored Corridon by naming a street after him. Frank Corridon Avenue abuts the old Freebody Park ball field, where he began his professional career, and is a little behind the Tennis Hall of Fame.

The Spitball

Perhaps Frank Corridon's most memorable contribution to the national pastime is the spitball. Although not well known nowadays, the spitball was as popular in the early twentieth century as the knuckleball is today. Research has failed to provide the answer to how Corridon threw the spitball, but there appear to be several methods of throwing the "spitter." The following is one such method. According to longtime Cranston resident and local Rhode Island baseball legend Neil Houston, the spitball pitch is performed by applying a large amount of a foreign substance, such as "chew," on the ball just prior to release. The weight from the glob of guck causes the ball to take "sort of an elliptical rotation," resulting in an irregular flight path. The ball tends to drop "off the table" near the plate or acts in some other unpredictable way. (Neil learned the pitch from an old-time ballplayer in the mid-1930s.)

Using a small amount of substance—which might or might not be spit—eliminates the typical spin on the ball, which results in the ball acting very much like the current-day knuckleball. When this form of spitball is thrown, the spin is all but eliminated, allowing the passage of air over and around the ball's seams to have a great effect on its path—a very unpredictable flight.

Whether Corridon is the actual inventor of the pitch is a matter of some debate, but this writer's research provides two points of support for this theory: (1) Corridon's name pops up in many sources as the inventor, and (2) the spitball was associated with Corridon as early as the mid-1890s, prior to any other discussion found in articles associated with the major leagues.

Local lore has it that Frank invented the spitball while a youngster playing sandlot games at the corner of Farewell Street and Van Zandt Avenue in Newport. Research by the late baseball historian Dick Thompson suggests a specific path the spitball took to get to the major leagues. Thompson notes, "Supposedly, George Hildebrand, an outfielder for the Boston Braves in 1902, watched Corridon warming up by licking his fingers. They talked about it, and the spitball made its major-league debut shortly thereafter. Hildebrand reportedly taught the spitball to Elmer Stricklett, the other pitcher sometimes credited with its invention." Thompson mentioned several other sources that strongly suggest Corridon as the inventor.

During Frank Corridon's career, the spitball remained "legal." In 1920, the pitch was outlawed by the owners, although pitchers were allowed to continue using the pitch until they retired. Major League Baseball commissioner Ford Frick tried to revive the pitch in 1955, but his proposal did not gain any momentum with the owners. However, the spitball and its derivatives remain in use—illegally—even today. Strangely, newspaper accounts during Corridon's career do not mention his use of the pitch. And although he is known as the inventor of the spitball, there is no indication that it was his primary pitch. Actually, according to contemporary accounts, his "out pitch" was a sneaky curveball. In addition to pitching, Corridon was also used by many teams as a center fielder.

George D. Donnelly: A True Sportsperson

Without community service, we would not have a strong quality of life. It's as important to the person who serves, as well as the recipient. It's the way in which we ourselves grow and develop.
—*Dorothy Height, social worker (1912–2010)*

There are many ways to help a community be healthy and strong. George D. Donnelly's way was through sports. He gave to his community tirelessly through his involvement with sports all his life without any expectation of return. In my opinion, that was what Dorothy Height was referring to in the quote above. Numerous references to Donnelly's generosity exist in news accounts during his many years of service. An electronic search of the Newport newspapers from 1925 through 1991 for "George D. Donnelly" reveals over 1,200 results, most of them referencing some way in which he volunteered in sports on behalf of the community. According to his son, George Donnelly Jr., he was so modest that he would not even allow the newspapers he wrote for to give him a byline. During his long life, he volunteered on community sports boards; coached teams; refereed and umpired games; was paramount in keeping the Sunset League in operation; assisted high school sports programs; shared his thoughts and wisdom through sports columns in the *Newport Herald, Newport Daily News* and *Providence Journal*; and, as his son put it, "was always down at Cardines Field helping someone." Although he shunned public recognition, he won many noteworthy awards, including the Frank Lanning Award for outstanding contributions to sports in Rhode Island, the 1970 Words Unlimited Award and the 1980 Media of the Year Award presented by the Rhode Island Association of Secondary School Athletic Directors.

Donnelly was a professional "old school" sportswriter. At the time of Donnelly's death in 1991, Dave Bloss, the sports editor for the *Providence Journal-Bulletin* sports editor, stated that he was "our eyes and ears in Newport...He went everywhere. Every event, he was there. He was the last of the old-guard 'stringers' in the classic sense of the word. He would clip his published stories, paste them together in

George Donnelly and his dog, Buddy, 1962. *Courtesy George Donnelly Jr.*

a string and send them in for payment." In 1927, at the age of twenty-five, Donnelly began writing for the *Newport Herald* and continued until the paper folded in 1946. He then began working for the *Newport Daily News*, writing a column called "Sports in the News" until his death at age eighty-seven. He also worked as a stringer for the *Providence Journal-Bulletin* during the 1950s. Largely self-taught, he wrote in a clear, interesting style and often included historical information in his articles. Because of his extensive coverage of high school sports and the help he provided students, St. George's School created the George D. Donnelly Award. The award is given to a student "who, in the opinion of the headmaster and the athletic directors, possesses a passion for athletics and who demonstrates dedication and sportsmanship and succeeds in a variety of athletic endeavors." George Donnelly was inducted into the Newport Sports Hall of Fame in 2002 and the St. George's Sports Hall of Fame in 2006.

Baseball and Other Sports Endeavors

George D. Donnelly was born on June 11, 1903, in Newport. Growing up, he played all sports. Coming into adulthood, he started playing in the Sunset League in 1922 and continued through 1939. His main position was catcher; however, he also played outfield and, when the need arose, pitched. He led the Sunset League in RBIs in 1931 and was runner-up in 1932 and 1933. He played for numerous teams during his career, including the Point Hummers, Red Men and Red Sox (a local Newport team). Donnelly was also an excellent basketball player, winning the Rhode Island Free Throw Competition three times in the late 1920s and early 1930s, which qualified him for national placement. Among the many sports teams he coached was the Boxwoods basketball team, which won the Rhode Island State Basketball Tournament in 1928, 1929 and 1930. (Author's note: The Sunset League is now named the George D. Donnelly Sunset League.)

The best description of how George Donnelly interacted professionally with the community comes from his son George Donnelly Jr.:

> *My dad kept himself mentally, physically and spiritually fit throughout his entire life. Amazingly, on the very day of his death, he had just completed his last "Sports in the News" column and submitted it to the newspaper. It appeared posthumously in the* Newport Daily News *the very next day.*

Catcher George Donnelly and the Newports, circa 1930. *Courtesy George Donnelly Jr.*

An interesting story appeared in the March 7, 1952 paper. There was a tiny clip in the newspaper mentioning "Mr. Donnelly's foul-shooting ability." The event took place down at the old "Hut," which is now called the Martin Recreation Center. Just for kicks, my father wanted to see if he still possessed the magic touch in shooting. His first shot missed, but the next thirty-six sailed through the hoop perfectly. His two-word description of such an accomplishment sums up his demeanor perfectly: "Just lucky."

He was an incredibly quiet man who never swore. (I know this is hard to believe, but it's true!) I can attest to a number of games I attended when heated arguments arose between players and umpires. Voices would become elevated, as foul language penetrated the night air, and coaches ran from the dugouts to push their weight around disputing a questionable call. Finally, they would approach the scorer's box to ask "Mr. Donnelly's" opinion. As you well know, disputes between scorekeepers often can be as heated and frequent as they are with an umpire on the field. Not in the Sunset League. "Saint Georges" simply would state the rules of whatever play was in question and, with a firm voice, say, "Let's get on with the game and play ball!" I don't ever recall a player or coach disputing my father's scoring decision. I was always impressed with that degree of respect.

Mr. Donnelly was the Sunset League's official scorer and statistician for more than fifty years. He believed in the importance of community, as evidenced by his many activities that helped youth and adults who lived within the borders of Newport. A visitor to Newport today would have no difficulty noticing the numerous ball fields and parks dispersed throughout the small city. One person who can be thanked for this is George D. Donnelly. He emphasized the importance of these community assets by providing excellent leadership as the director of the Newport Recreation Department from 1943 until his retirement in 1969. Throughout his tenure, he helped to ensure that the existing parks were maintained and that other public areas were developed. No community can be healthy without a good amount of green space and areas dedicated to the physical activity and enjoyment of its residents. Every community needs a patron such as George D. Donnelly. Throughout his eighty-seven years as a Newport resident, he continually demonstrated his commitment to community service. Newport is much better off because of his efforts.

Chapter 7

NEWPORT, THE MILITARY AND BASEBALL

Baseball and the military have enjoyed a symbiotic relationship since the Revolutionary War. "Ball," most likely a form of town ball, was played at Valley Forge. As baseball was developed in the first part of the nineteenth century, a primary vehicle used to spread the game was the military. During this time, the country was becoming nationalized. Army and navy personnel came from all parts of the civilized country to serve and culturally integrated within the armed forces. As young men were thrown together into camps and on ships, they learned the game now called baseball. For as long as there has been humanity and civilization, there have been armed forces. When not in battle, drilling or marching, "down time" was spent playing games of all sorts. Baseball became one of the most popular games because it was a team sport, and the army and navy were, in essence, divided into units that lent themselves into developing teams. Early in the 1800s, before the invention of basketball and football in America, cricket and baseball were the only large-scale team games in town. Cricket, while popular among certain young men, was still considered a "gentleman's game" from England, carrying with it the resentment of the aristocracy of nobility so disdained by the "commoners" in the United Sates. During the Civil War, baseball was introduced to many Union soldiers who had come from points out west and had not yet become familiar with the game that had originated and was played mainly in the eastern and southern parts of the country. Many Confederate soldiers learned the game from Union prisoners. From the Gray and the Blue, the game was brought back to every backwater nook and cranny in rural America, where it spread quickly after the war. After the Civil War, baseball blossomed and became popular in almost every locality, town and city in America.

During baseball's formative years, the game proliferated in many cities throughout the East, South and West, even reaching as far as California and Hawaii. Alexander Cartwright literally taught the game in his westward travels, and through the symbiotic relationship with the military, the game wove its way into the tapestry of our society. Everywhere the military went, baseball followed.

Starting after the Revolutionary War, the newly formed federal government began to develop military installations for defense and training up and down Narragansett Bay and especially in Newport. This contributed significantly to the numerous military baseball teams that would come to populate the area. The earthworks at Fort Adams, located in the old settlement of Brenton Village, were developed by Lieutenant Colonel Totten starting on August 10, 1825, as part of the coastal defense system. There is no doubt that baseball in its rudimentary form soon followed. Later, Goat Island and Coasters Harbor Island followed suit. Our story focuses on the baseball teams that came with these developments.

The Torpedo Station, the Naval Training Station and the Sunset League: A Tale of Two Teams

The Torpedo Station opened on Goat Island in July 1869. Although I found no written records of baseball being played that early at the Torpedo Station, the sport definitely would have been played, at least in its pickup-game form. The Naval Training Station officially opened in 1883 on Coasters Harbor Island. The first written record I could find of a baseball team from either location indicated that a team from the Naval Training Station played the Newports in 1881. This early baseball team is quite remarkable, considering that it played before there was an official Naval Training Station.

In the February 12, 1881 edition of the *Newport Daily News*, the following appeared under the caption "The Training Station":

> *It will be seen by the following telegram from Hartford, Connecticut, to the* New York Herald *of Friday that Newport is not to have the Naval*

AMERICA'S PASTIME IN THE CITY BY THE SEA

Training Station without a struggle. Both branches of the Connecticut legislature today passed a resolution directing Senators and Representatives of the state in Congress to use earnest and determined efforts to prevent the removal of the United States Naval Training Station from the Thames River, 4 miles above New London.

Both Rhode Island's and Connecticut's state legislative bodies were hard at work the following year. Many news accounts indicated a back-and-forth effect regarding which state would get the station. The September 2, 1882 edition of the *Newport Mercury* finally reported the navy's decision: "On Saturday last, Secretary of the Navy Chandler visited Coasters Harbor Island and formally took possession of the site for the United States Naval Training Station."

The Naval Training Station officially opened in 1883, two years after the previously mentioned game between the Naval Training Station team and the Newports. The Naval War College also was established in 1885 on Coasters Harbor Island and had a graduating class of nine students that year. Regarding the Naval Training Station baseball team of 1881, a small mystery exists. Apparently, the U.S. Navy had informally established the station a year before the official takeover. Regardless, there would be a Naval

A run-down ball field on Coasters Island, 2002. *Photo credit author.*

Training Station team every year going forward from 1881 to the present day. The baseball field on Coasters Harbor Island remains active to this day. There have been several locations for the ballpark, including one at the entrance, one in front of the artillery practice field in the early 1900s and the run-down but still visible field in the middle of the island.

Both the Torpedo Station and the Naval Training Station played baseball throughout the 1880s and '90s and into the twentieth century before joining the Sunset League in 1920s. Prior to becoming involved with the Sunset League, both stations fielded formidable teams against college, amateur, semipro and professional minor-league and major-league teams. Once they joined the Sunset League, the two teams went on very different courses, creating the "tale of two teams."

The Torpedo Station, unlike the Naval Training Station and the Naval War College, was a hands-on environment where torpedoes of all sorts were designed and tested. Even in modern times, a fishing boat's crew will occasionally be surprised by the mammoth munition "catch of the day"—a real live torpedo of some indistinguishable vintage. These catches can bite back if the torpedo is not necessarily disarmed. The experiences and backgrounds of these fishermen were different than those of the personnel at the Naval Training Station and the Naval War College. However, they shared the great American sport called baseball. But while they certainly weren't bad teams, they did not share the success of their military neighbors.

The Torpedo Station team joined the Sunset League in 1922 and remained engaged off and on until 1951, playing a total of twenty-one years. During these years, the team won two championships and compiled a record of 219-274, a .444 winning percentage. The best years were 1922 (16-4), 1923 (16-4), 1930 (15-9), 1935 (17-6) and 1943 (24-6). The team's worst year was 1951, when it went 1-22 for a .043 winning percentage.

The Naval Training Station team fared considerably better in the win column. It joined the Sunset League in 1923 and over the next three years went 19-8, 21-4 and 16-9 for a .727 winning percentage. The team also won either the first-half or the second-half pennant three years running and took the championship in 1925. Its success did not end there, however, as it won the championship three out of its last five years in the league: 1951, 1953 and 1954. Between 1951 and 1954, the Naval Training Station team posted 70 wins against 24 losses for a .745 winning percentage. Overall, the Naval Training Station team played thirteen seasons between 1923 and 1958 and compiled a remarkable record of 188-105 for a winning percentage of .641—an excellent record in any league.

Every Ship Had a Team

By the late 1800s and early 1900s, just about every ship in the U.S. Navy fleet had a baseball team. They played for the Atlantic Fleet Championship, the Pacific Fleet Championship and a host of other naval base championships. Whenever a ship docked, its team played the locals. Unfortunately, one of these ships, the USS *Maine*, became famous for the wrong reason when it blew up while anchored in Havana Harbor. The incident was blamed on sabotage, led to the creation of the battle cry "Remember the Maine!" and brought on the Spanish-American War. (It is now believed that the explosion was caused by a faulty boiler.)

Just before the sinking, the *Maine*'s baseball team had won the 1898 North Atlantic Squadron Championship. The simple fact that there was a "championship" series involving a navy squadron this early illustrates the level of popularity the game had in the service at the time. The only member of the team shown in the photograph on the following pages to survive the explosion was J.H. Bloomer (top left, standing). Also, of special note is that the pitcher of the team, William Lambert, was black. To overcome the inherent institutional discrimination of the period and assume such a prominent position on the team, he must have been one heck of a pitcher.

USS *New Hampshire*, 1900. *Author's collection.*

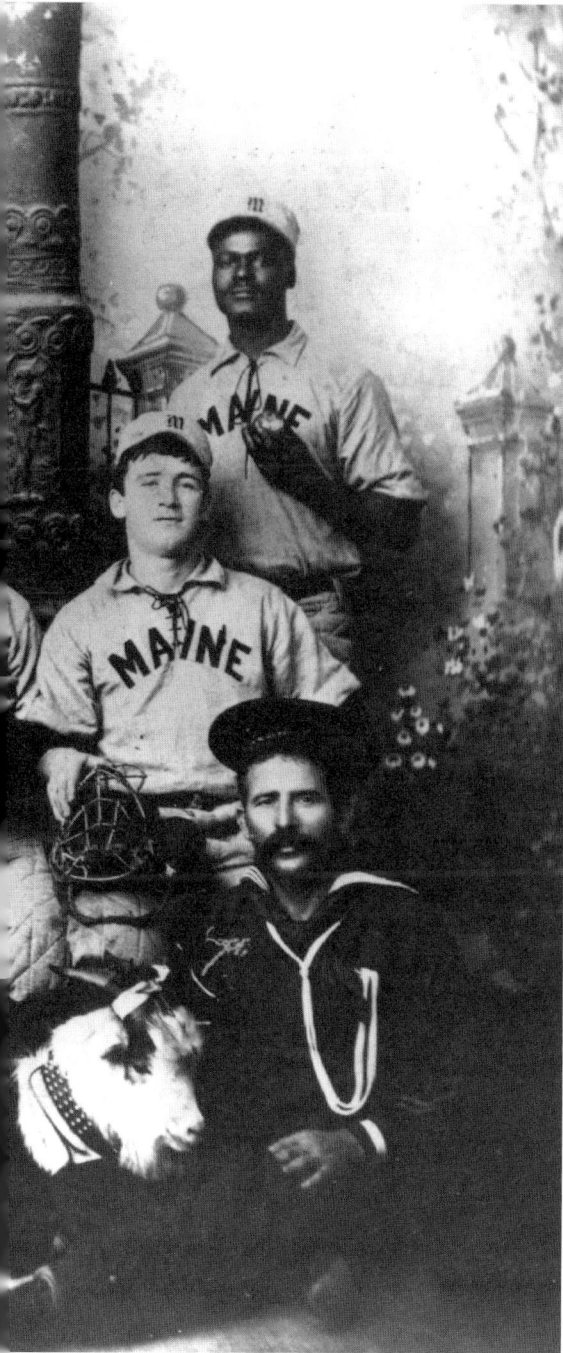

Many of the navy teams were quite good, as illustrated by the Naval Training Station's squads. It was difficult for a ship to consistently sponsor a really good team because crews were constantly changing, and finding time for practice was difficult. However, this was overcome somewhat by sailors practicing on deck.

Following is a list of U.S. Navy ship teams that played baseball in Newport as of this writing:

USS *Arcadia*
USS *Bailey*
USS *Cascade*
USS *Constellation*
USS *Davisville*
USS *Dionysus*
USS *Dobbin*
USS *Louisiana*
USS *Markab*
USS *New Hampshire*
USS *Puget Sound*
USS *Rappahanock*
USS *Vestal*
USS *Vulcan*
USS *Whitney*
USS *Yellowstone*
USS *Yosemite*
USS *Washington*

The USS *Maine* baseball team one month before the ship was sunk in Cuba. Note that the pitcher is African American. 1898. *Courtesy Library of Congress LC-USZ62-26149.*

Baseball practice on unknown aircraft carrier, circa 1939. *Author's collection.*

USS *Louisiana*, 1900. *Author's collection.*

FORT ADAMS

Baseball most likely was played at Fort Adams before the Civil War, but there is no written documentation to back up this speculation. The first report I could find for a baseball game played by a Fort Adams team was written in 1892. This game took place on the Naval Training Station grounds on Coasters Harbor Island between a team simply called Ship and an opponent called the Forts. The following report appeared in the May 30, 1892 *Newport Daily News*:

> *At the Training Station Saturday the Ship's nine defeated one representing Fort Adams. Tehan pitched for the ship and struck out 15 men in six innings of play. The umpire came from the Fort and evidently "made a mistake" in his calling. The sides were as follows: Ship—Tehan, Rogers, Sweeney, Denniston, Cunningham, Bartley, Martin, McDonnell, and Minster. Forts—Hoover, Parker, Echels, McDermott, Hackett, O'Brien, Logan, Smith, and Jantey. Outside of their inability to hit Tehan, the Forts put up a good game, showing the presence of good individual players. The score:*

Innings	1	2	3	4	5	6	
Ship	2	0	3	1	0	0	6
Fort	1	0	0	0	0	4	5

Harbor scene from Fort Adams, circa 1908. *Author's collection.*

Left: A Fort Adams player, circa 1920. *Author's collection.*

Below: The 130th baseball team with children at Fort Adams, circa 1918. *Author's collection.*

A baseball game being played at Fort Adams, circa 1920. *Author's collection.*

The Providence Grays and Sandy Hook heritage teams after their game at Fort Adams, 2013. *Courtesy and photo credit Peter Oppenheimer.*

As stated earlier, one can learn a lot from a box score, even a rudimentary one such as this. (One must also use the brief write-up, for it is almost like part of the box score.) We see that there were fifteen strikeouts by the Ship's pitcher. The game went six innings, and the Ship team would've felt very comfortable through five innings but must have been sweating bullets in the bottom of the sixth. We can learn the approximate location of the game, and we can also pick up on the reporter's sarcastic humor regarding the umpire. One might also speculate on the possible ethnicity of the teams—which in this case is Irish, with ten of sixteen players having Irish surnames.

Baseball continued to be played by Fort Adams teams until the fort was decommissioned and developed into a wonderful park after World War II. Since then, it has been used for many events, most notably the Newport Jazz and Folk Festivals.

WORLD WAR I, NEWPORT, TEDDY ROOSEVELT, FRANK GILMORE AND THE SECOND NAVAL DISTRICT BASE BALL CLUB

By 1917, the U.S. Navy was gearing up for war, and Newport was being inundated by a never-ending tide of sailors stationed and training at Newport's two naval sites. Regardless of location, wherever there is a military base, a tension develops between the local residents and military personnel. This was especially true in Newport when the nation became embroiled in World War I. And these tensions did not go unnoticed by one of Newport's favorite visitors, ex-president Theodore "Teddy" Roosevelt. To help mitigate these tensions, Roosevelt established a baseball team, the Second Naval District Base Ball Club, which was composed of sailors from the submarine base in Newport. The navy hired ex–major leaguer and Newport native Frank Corridon to manage the team. The Second Naval District team turned out to be a very good one, defeating most opponents it played. The team battled the Class-A minor-league Providence Grays, Boston College, Brown University, Princeton, the New York Giants, West Point, Camp Devens and Fort Adams, as well as local amateur and semipro teams. Among the team's players was a young, scrappy submariner and native Rhode Islander named Frank Gilmore. Gilmore had played in the Connecticut State League in 1915 and was a member of the Providence Grays in 1916.

Teddy Roosevelt (right) in Newport, circa 1918. *Courtesy George Donnelly Jr.*

When Frank Gilmore enlisted in the navy in 1917, he figured to see action in the war. According to his grandson, John Gilmore, this never came to be. He was assigned to the submarine base, and when Teddy Roosevelt started the Second District Base Ball Club, he was immediately nabbed to play right field. Like other team members at the base, he never saw action during the war.

After Gilmore served his time, he settled in Johnston, Rhode Island, and began working at the Centerdale Worsted Company. It wasn't long before he started playing on the mill's team, and he immediately became its star player. After a couple seasons, he was earning a good salary and no longer had to work much in the shop. His job? Pitch every Sunday. Baseball wasn't the only "game" he played, however. He was such a celebrity that he started to develop business contacts at the games. When Prohibition was lifted in 1933, he started a liquor distributing business and became quite wealthy. Grandson John Gilmore remembers that his grandfather's home was frequented by many major-league players and the who's who of Rhode Island baseball. One of Frank's brothers, John Gilmore, played in the minor leagues with the Fort Wayne and Pawtucket teams in 1914–15.

LIKE THE THEME FROM SESAME STREET, "MILITARY BASEBALL TEAMS AND NEWPORT ARE FRIENDS"

Military baseball teams and Newport have had a relationship as long as baseball has existed. Determining how long that relationship has lasted depends on what theory of baseball's origin one subscribes to. It matters not whether one believes in what I like to refer to as the "folksong" (baseball developed over a long period, with many different contributors) or the "Alexander Cartwright theory" (baseball originated with the codifying of rules in 1845 by Cartwright), this "friendship" has lasted a long time. Military baseball teams and Newport share a common historic tapestry that dates back well over 150 years. Each team, each game, each at-bat, each pitch, each play and, most importantly, each fan reaction is a thread that is woven into the storyline of Newport history. The surface has barely been scratched in this chapter, and while it would be nice to linger, it is time to move on to other destinations within the covers of this book.

Chapter 8

Extra Innings

Extra Innings is sort of the "odds and ends" section of this book—home to items that don't fit anywhere else but are still relevant in this context.

The George Donnelly Sunset League

The Sunset League is the oldest amateur baseball league in the country, having been established in 1919 by Dr. Peter Intreglia. A total of 151 teams have participated in the league. The league is so named because originally there were no lights and each game had to end at sunset. It is truly amazing that the league has held together for so long through seven wars, several devastating hurricanes, the Great Depression and a slew of recessions. Year in, year out, the league has been a constant in Newport, providing pleasure for its residents, baseball teams and tourists.

The Sunset League has played in three ballparks: the Basin (Cardines), Freebody Park and the Wellington Grounds. For most of its existence, the Sunset League has called Cardines Field home. The league maintained its original name even though lights were installed at Cardines in 1938. However, it once again went dark during World War II (1942–45) for fear of attracting German U-boats.

Throughout the years, the Sunset League has used a couple different formats to establish championships. Sometimes it was a playoff series,

A Sunset League player, circa 1930. *Courtesy George Donnelly Jr.*

Opposite: Cover of the *Sunset Baseball League Record Book, 1919–1940. Courtesy George Donnelly Jr.*

sometimes there was a first-half champion and a second-half champion and sometimes there was simply a pennant. The title "Little World Series" has been used by teams and leagues throughout the twentieth century (especially in the 1950s) to signify a championship series. Sometimes the title was used by barnstorming teams that had played the actual World Series or to describe a series between two minor-league opponents. Most often, however, it was used for national semipro championship series. There is one instance in which the Sunset League hosted a Little World Series. The year was 1930. The record of this game is an excellent example of small-city reporting for baseball games. The whole article ran considerably more than a column (the length of the paper); however, a sample of the story will give the reader an idea of the style. Of course, at the center of the action is our hero, George Donnelly, playing right field and going two for four on the day. The following excerpt is from the September 12, 1930 edition of the *Newport Mercury and Weekly News*:

SUNSET BASEBALL LEAGUE

Record Book

1919 - 1940

Compiled and Edited

by

GEORGE D. DONNELLY

Official Scorer

———

PRICE   -   -   15 CENTS

POINT HUMMERS WIN THE CHAMPIONSHIP
DEFEAT FRANKLIN DRUG NINE BY SCORE OF 6–5
"LITTLE WORLD SERIES" BROUGHT TO A SUDDEN DEATH
DREAM OF GEORGE DONNELLY IS REALIZED

The Championship Crown of the Sunset League was placed on the brow of
the Point Hummers Sunday afternoon, and the "Little World Series" was

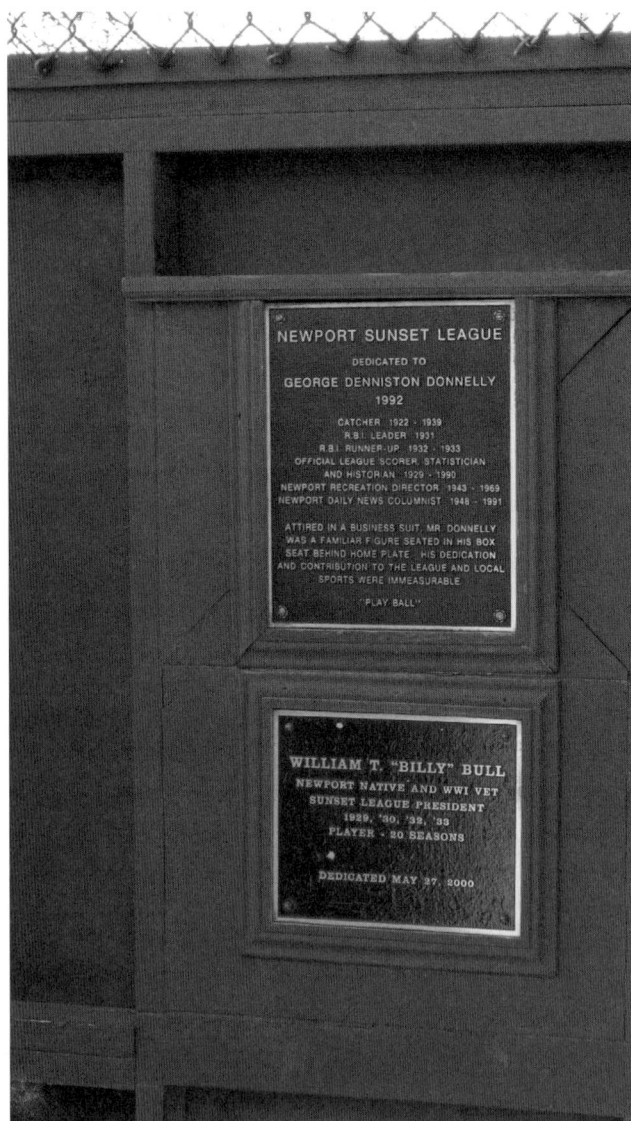

Dedication plaques at
Cardines Field, 2013.
Photo credit author.

brought to a sudden death. The dream of one George "Katzman" Donnelly was brought to life when the determined right fielder of the Hummers, and former catcher of Mac's Spa, shattered the hopes of Bill Cooper and the desires of the Franklin Drug nine by slapping a sharp single into right field in the first half of the eighth inning, with the bases loaded, two men out and his team one run in the rear. As the poet said, "Young blood must run its course, lad, and every dog his day." So yesterday was Donnelly's day, and his work of the season, as he plodded along under the most trying circumstances, was fittingly rewarded with the "blow that killed father." The final score of the contest was 6 to 5.

Because of the decision at second base in the last half of the inning by Umpire-in-Chief Stewart Leary, when he called out Oxx, who had attempted to advance second on a play at third, the Franklin nine played the remainder of the game under protest. Why they protested, no one knows. Oxx was out by a city block. There was no question about it, and the protest looked like the last resort of a drowning man grasping for a straw.

In 2019, the Sunset League will turn one hundred years old, and there is no reason not to expect the league to continue for another century after that. It certainly is not easy for an amateur league to last as long as the Sunset League has. It has taken dedicated individuals like George Donnelly, a dedicated city like Newport and a long tradition of baseball to maintain the league's vibrancy for a century. So, when in season, head on down to Newport and catch a Sunset League game. See some great baseball as it should be played, and become part of tradition that is baseball in Newport!

To learn more about the George Donnelly Sunset League, go to www. gdsunsetleague.com. This website contains schedules and a wealth of historical information, including records for every season since 1919.

A Year in the Life of Early Newport Baseball—1892

One way to understand a community's relationship with baseball in the early days of the sport is to review every page of the most prominent local newspaper and retrieve every game. This allows the researcher—and eventually you, the reader—to gain a comprehension of certain aspects of that community. We can learn from the names of the teams and players, as well as from the number/types of teams in relation to population.

The year 1892 was an exciting time to be in America. Underlying what has been referred to as the lively and mislabeled frivolous Gay Nineties actually was a tremendous era of growth in technology, social justice and entertainment. It was a time of development of the "helping professionals" (e.g., social work and psychology), great inventions, entrepreneurism, quantum leaps in communications, creation of brand-new sports and much more. Wonder and change were all around, and the groundwork was being laid for the new century. In 1892:

- Ellis Island, located in the waters off Manhattan, was opened as the reception center for new immigrants.
- In Massachusetts, the rules of basketball were published in *Triangle Magazine* and the first basketball game was played.
- Lord Stanley presented the first silver challenge cup for hockey. The cup, originally known as the Dominion Hockey Challenge Cup, was renamed the Stanley Cup in 1893.
- George C. Blickensderfer patented the portable typewriter, greatly increasing the work capacity of writers.
- The General Electric Company was incorporated in New York.
- The first Sunday National League baseball game was played. The Cincinnati Reds beat the St. Louis Browns 5–1.
- Charles Duryea drove the first American-made automobile. Duryea engineered the first American gas-powered car and was co-founder of the Duryea Motor Wagon Company, America's first automobile company.
- African American longshoremen went on strike for higher wages in St. Louis, Missouri.
- Charlie Reilly became baseball's first pinch-hitter.
- George Sampson patented the first clothes dryer.
- Dr. Washington Sheffield invented the toothpaste tube.
- The Sierra Club was formed in San Francisco by the great naturalist John Muir in order to conserve nature.
- African American Homer A. Plessy refused to go to a segregated railroad car, an action that resulted in the lawsuit *Plessy v. Ferguson*. As a result of the suit, the U.S .Supreme Court established the "Separate But Equal" doctrine. The 1892 ruling remained in effect

until 1954, when it was overturned by the Supreme Court decision in *Brown v. Board of Education.*

- Wilbert Robinson set a baseball record by going seven for seven in a nine-inning game, an achievement that wasn't equaled until Rennie Stennett did the same on September 16, 1975. No major-league player has ever had eight hits in a nine-inning game.

- The Salvation Army Limelight Department, one of the world's first film studios, was officially established in Melbourne, Australia. Between 1892 and 1909, the Limelight Department made more than three hundred films to promote religion.

- Sunday school teacher Lizzie Borden was arrested in Fall River, Massachusetts, for the axe murders of her parents. She was found innocent by a jury. The case remains unsolved.

- James Corbett knocked out the great John L. Sullivan in twenty-one rounds to win the heavyweight boxing title. "Gentleman Jim" Corbett was the first boxer to apply science to the sport. This match was also the first one in which boxers used gloves in the ring.

- The first public appearance of the great bandleader John Philip Sousa's band took place. (Historical Note: John Philip Sousa credited David W. Reeves as one of his inspirational mentors. Reeves composed many marches and was the leader of Rhode Island's own American Band, the oldest incorporated community band in the country (established in 1837 and still performing today). The American Band often opened baseball games for Newport teams and still holds summer concerts on the beach in Newport. I rank the three most important community organizations in nineteenth- and early twentieth-century communities as—in this order—baseball, community bands and religious establishments. Many baseball games in Rhode Island were opened by local community bands.)

- The Diamond Match Co. patented book matches.

- In Mansfield, Pennsylvania, the first night football game was played.

- The first commercial long-distance phone line was strung, opening direct and instantaneous communication between Chicago and New York City.

- Arthur Conan Doyle published *The Adventures of Sherlock Holmes.*

- Pudge Heffelfinger received $500 and became the first professional football player.

- Anti-Semite Hermann Ahlwardt was elected to Germany's Reichstag, helping to set the stage for the horrible actions of the mid-twentieth century.
- Peter Ilyich Tchaikovsky's ballet *Nutcracker Suite* had its premiere.
- The pneumatic automobile tire was invented in Syracuse, New York, paving the way (no pun intended) for the continued development of the automobile. Without these tires, cars would literally have been shaken apart by the roads of the time period.
- North Carolina Biddle defeated Livingston 4–0 in the first all-black college football game.

Of course, there were many other events in 1892. Listing these few gives the reader a sense of the breadth of changes taking place. In all of my writings, I strive to maintain a sense of baseball's place within the historical context of "all levels of community" as experienced by the individuals of the time period covered. Now, back to baseball in Newport in 1892.

TEAMS

According to written documentation, Newport hosted at least eleven teams in 1892. These included the Atlantics and Pacifics, both of which were semiprofessional teams, as well as four military teams: Fort Adams, Battery B, The Ship and the Naval Training Station. In addition, five amateur teams were reported: the Summer Residents, the Bachelors, the Benedicts, the Banner Boys and Rogers High School. Similarities and differences exist regarding the types of teams when compared to other Rhode Island communities. The Summer Residents and the military teams would not be found in other communities and were strictly representative of the nature of Newport. It was very common to find two or three semiprofessional teams in communities the size of Newport in the early 1890s. No Rhode Island community of the time would be complete without a game between the Bachelors and Benedicts. (Although not listed as an origin of this slang word on the Internet, where I grew up in the Midwest, "Benedict" was a reference to the traitor Benedict Arnold, signifying the feelings of the remaining bachelors in town having been "betrayed." I speculate that this was meant to humorlessly insult the "weakness of the newly married man.") (Note: The 1880s and '90s saw a humorous levity applied to the game of baseball.

Besides the Bachelors and Benedicts, most communities also hosted games between the Heavyweights and the Lightweights and the Brunettes and Blondes, even games in which all or some of the men playing were dressed as women.)

A Not-So-Well-Written Account of the Game Between the Bachelors and Benedicts— Newport Style (as reported in the July 20, 1892 edition of the *Newport Daily News*)

This account is presented to the reader without benefit of edits or clarifications to demonstrate a common writing style of the time period associated with small-circulation newspapers.

BACHELORS *vs.* BENEDICTS
An Interesting Game of Ball at Morton Park

Married men vs. single, and all artists, at baseball, was an announcement that drew a good sized crowd gathering to Morton Park yesterday afternoon. As had been intimated in the News, when the game was first announced, there were suspicious circumstances connected with the preliminaries that led those experienced in sporting matters to think that the Benedicts were putting up a game, other than ball, on their unsuspecting brothers who had did not experience the joys and sorrows of married life. It is expected that Managers Martin and Corbett would do better work for their side in objecting to any good players on the opposition nine than they could possibly do in the field, and they did. The full extent of their scheming was not, however, appreciated until the victims perceived the Greene goods that was sprung upon them. It was considered only just to have two umpires, one married, the other single; the latter was Jack Tobin, of the Atlantics, who having a regard for the game, umpired squarely throughout, his only objectionable act being the fining the Manager Martin one cigar; the former was Fred W Greene, who is usually attractive appearance, was increased by handsome silk umbrella. No one at first knew why he carried this, and as there was no umbrella dealers on the Benedicts team, the truth was not suspected until the game was well underway. There was no questions in the minds of the spectators but that the Bachelors had been sold at a snap auction, without being given an opportunity to bid.

This is a good example of the everyday writing style of the period of a small daily newspaper. There are seventeen commas/semicolons in the short writing sample, creating long run-on sentences that are hard to follow. In addition, the mystery of the umbrella is never addressed in the rest of article, so you would had to have been there to understand the reference. The full coverage for this game runs a column and a half, or approximately one thousand words. Truly, the article is very difficult to read and says very little. What can be garnered from the article is that the score was 27–22 in favor of the Benedicts, that there were so many errors due to clowning around that the scorekeeper chose not to record them and that Greene, the "married" umpire, called an irregular game with comedy in mind and did something with this fancy umbrella. Also, the players appeared to have had more fun than the spectators, as demonstrated by the end of the article: "At the end of the seventh inning nearly all the spectators had disappeared, leaving two bank treasurers, a bank cashier and small boys to enjoy the picnic of the last two innings."

The article went on to state that the police were disappointed in not having to break up fights or to have to call for the ambulances. In reality, the policemen were probably happy that they did not have to get involved, for many games of the 1880s and '90s commonly ended in a brawl between the two teams, hence the reference to the ambulances and the police in the article. In more serious games, when a brawl ensued, the team winning the brawl would often confiscate the equipment of the opposing team. This process is well described in an article in an 1888 *Cranston Ledger* in which the Atlantics of Cranston were described as the strongest team, in a literal sense, and also the best equipped.

Rogers High School

Rogers High School was officially founded in 1873 by educator William Sanford Rogers. The first news coverage of the school that can be found appeared in the June 3, 1872 edition of the *Newport Daily News*: "[T] he Trustees are authorized and directed to pay to Brown University one thousand dollars for a scholarship for the benefit of such graduates of Rogers

Newly built Rogers High School, 1884. *Author's collection.*

High School as may be designated by the Superintendent with the consent of the aforementioned Trustees." It may be assumed that baseball was being played by Rogers students shortly thereafter. Rogers High School has had many great players and teams. The 1892 team is an excellent example. Rogers played its first game of the season on April 24 against a "Picked Nine" composed of adult players of semiprofessional status. Rogers won that game 9–4. The high school team posted two more victories against the Naval Training Station in May, winning 15–2 and 8–0.

In June, the team suffered two defeats, one at the hands of the Pacifics, 4–2, and the other to Friends School (now Moses Brown) of Providence, 13–11. However, Rogers came roaring back, beating the semipro Jamestown Stars by a score of 10–4 and defeating a "Picked Nine" 15–12. In the next two months, the team defeated two more semipro teams, the Atlantics (6–2) and the Stars (22–9 and 9–6). On August 2, Rogers defeated Battery B 14–1. In its last game of the season, on August 15, Rogers lost 12–5 to the Stars.

At any level of baseball, it would have been considered a great season. Rogers High School had gone 9-3 for a winning percentage of .750. The team had scored 112 runs against opponents' 68 for a very healthy run differential of forty-four runs in twelve games. The most amazing part of this winning season was that only one game was against another high school team. The rest of the games were against adult teams, and in seven of those games, the teams were composed of semiprofessional players. Given these factors, any coach at any level would be extremely pleased with the season's outcome.

It should be noted that in its long baseball history, Rogers has produced many great players, two of whom played in the major leagues. One was Frank Corridon, who made his major-league debut on April 15, 1904, pitching for the Chicago Nationals (Cubs) against the Philadelphia Phillies. The other was pitcher Pat Combs, who was drafted eleventh overall by the Phillies in 1988 and made his major-league debut against the Pittsburgh Pirates on September 5, 1989.

THE REMAINING TEAMS

Both of the semiprofessional teams, the Pacifics and the Atlantics, primarily played other semipro teams from Massachusetts in 1892. The Atlantics were the weaker of the two teams, compiling a record of 3-4 in 7 games. The Pacifics club played 17 games. This team was excellent, posting a record of 14-3 for a winning percentage of .824. Despite their excellent record, the team's run differential was not good, generally just one to three runs per game. However, the Pacifics appeared to have a knack for scoring a lot of runs when they needed to and, at other times, holding their opponents to a low number of runs when they themselves scored few runs. There was little coverage of the other teams that played in Newport in 1892. Battery B, Summer Residents, Fort Adams and a military team simply referred to as "Ship" are covered just once; the Banner Boys twice; and the Naval Training Station just three times. All teams playing that summer in Newport shared a common factor: their games were all well attended, and they were supported by the public.

1892 Recap

Here is a summary of our one-year microscopic study of early baseball in Newport. In 1892, Newport supported quite a number of teams with a mixture of semipro, military, amateur and high school teams. The paid attendance was good enough to bring in teams from as far as way as Roxbury, Massachusetts. All games appear to have been played at Morton Park. The high school team had to be one of the best in the state, given its record against adult semipro teams. It is noteworthy that unlike other Rhode Island communities, no mill teams played in Newport during this time. And finally, the sportswriting wasn't of the highest quality.

Black Ball in Rhode Island and Newport

Unfortunately, the viable written record for how black men and women in Rhode Island played the game is extremely limited. There is no doubt that baseball was an important part of black history in the Ocean State, but due to institutional discrimination, the story remains largely undocumented and certainly untold. As of this writing, the earliest recorded date found for black baseball being played in Rhode Island was August 17, 1877, when the Rhode Islands played the Mutual Club of Washington, D.C. According to Robert Cvornyek, chair of the Rhode Island College History Department and a historian of black baseball, the Mutuals were a traveling black team composed mostly of office workers who were members of the Freedmen's Bureau. The game was won by the Rhode Islands, 6–0.

The first African American to play on a major-league team might have been a Rhode Islander. Whether that is so depends on how one defines race and ethnicity. Baseball historians have long considered that Moses Fleetwood Walker was the first African American player in the major leagues. In 1884, Walker played for Toledo of the American Association, a major league at the time. After the 1884 season, Walker was released and never played in the major leagues again, nor did any other African American until Jackie Robinson in 1947.

William Edward White, however, might have preceded Walker. White, who played in one game for the Providence Grays of the National League in 1879, was born in 1860 to a biracial mother who was a slave to A.J. White, a railroad president and wealthy plantation owner in Milner, Georgia. Thanks to the excellent research of SABR member Peter Morris, we know that White was 25 percent black and 75 percent white. By the definitions of the time, he would have been classified as black. We do not know if he was born a slave or a free person.

White, who started at first base for the Brown University varsity team, played with the Grays on June 21, 1879. By contemporary standards, he would have been the first black man to play in major-league baseball. By today's standards, however, White could classify himself as white, black or biracial. In my opinion, Mr. White was the best authority to identify his racial heritage, especially given the blatant racial discrimination of his time, even in the North. Mr. White chose his own path in the 1880 census when he marked "white" as his racial heritage. Determining whether he was the first black man to play baseball in the majors is a matter of definition and depends on the perspective of the person making the determination.

The honor of being the most distinguished black baseball player from Rhode Island has to go to one William A. Heathman, Esquire. Heathman attended Brown University in 1891–92 and played on the varsity baseball team. He transferred to Boston University, where he obtained a law degree. Moving back to Rhode Island after graduation, he became the first black man to be admitted to the Rhode Island Bar Association. He was the first black person to be admitted to practice before the U.S. Circuit Court (1901) and the first black person to serve as a clerk for the Rhode Island Supreme Court. Heathman lived to be over ninety and practiced law until his death.

AMERICA'S PASTIME IN THE CITY BY THE SEA

Several traveling black teams played in Rhode Island in the 1880s through the 1950s, including the famous Cuban Giants of the late nineteenth century. Among others were the Pullman Porters, the Black Yankees and the New England Black Giants

An early black baseball team in Rhode Island was the Providence Colored Grays, who played the Pascoags on September 9, 1886. The Colored Grays were shorthanded and lost to an excellent semipro Pascoag team, 13–3. This game was umpired by an African American gentleman named Mr. Howard. Howard may have been the first black umpire to officiate in a game with white players in Rhode Island.

The longest-running black team in Rhode Island was the Providence Colored Giants, who began playing sometime prior to 1902 and existed until at least 1932. Daniel Whitehead ran the team from 1902 to 1932. The last owner of the team was Arthur "Daddy" Black, who was murdered on the evening of September 24, 1932, by five black men from New York City. Black was shot down in his own home in a blaze of gunfire. Besides being owner of the Providence Colored Giants, he was a numbers runner and illegal lottery promoter.

Newport was also host to many traveling teams. These teams usually played at the old Polo Grounds or Freebody Park in the late nineteenth century, at Wellington Park in the early twentieth century and, later, at Cardines Field. On August 24, 1909, Newport even hosted the traveling Cherokee Indian team at the Wellington Grounds. In addition to hosting traveling teams, Newport was also home to a number of black baseball teams throughout the years. (Reminder: This data is very incomplete due to a lack of written reports.) (Information credit: Robert Cvornyek.)

Newports—1879
Newports—1883
Puritans—1886
Resolutes—1887
Newport Colored Giants—1931
Newport Union Athletic Club—1932
Union Athletic Club—1932

BARNSTORMING TEAMS COME TO NEWPORT

House of David

The Israelite House of David was a religious society founded by Benjamin and Mary Purnell in Benton Harbor, Michigan, in 1903. The House of David developed a high-quality baseball team sometime between 1913 and 1915. By the 1920s, the team was barnstorming across the country and often included such baseball stars as Grover Cleveland Alexander, Satchel Paige and Mordecai Brown, all future Hall of Famers. The House of David was all about great baseball and entertainment. Not unlike the Harlem Globetrotters of today, the players would put on a show, sometimes with the major-league players joining in the act and dressing up as women while playing. The most outstanding characteristic of the players—aside from their baseball skills— was their long hair and long beards, as the religious society forbid them from trimming. In 1935, the House of David split into two factions, each sponsoring traveling baseball teams. House of David teams continued to barnstorm through 1955, appearing often at special events such as carnivals and state fairs. There was even an all-black House of David traveling team that played exclusively in the Negro Leagues.

The House of David baseball teams began coming to Newport in the late 1930s and continued through to visit until the early 1950s. They played

House of David baseball players, 1930. *Author's collection.*

primarily at Cardines Field, facing various Sunset League All-Star teams from Newport. The House of David played an honest, rough form of baseball that one would classify as "old school." In July 1940, pitcher Ross of the Sunset League suffered a fractured skull when he was hit by a brush-back pitch. Remarkably, he continued to pitch the rest of the game. This is a well-known story in Newport baseball lore. Not known at all, however, is the story of twelve-year-old Carl Oliver, as told in the July 15, 1940 edition of the *Newport Mercury and Weekly News*: "Wednesday evening at a floodlight game at Cardines Field, Carl Oliver, 12, of 31 Catherine St., received a head injury when he was hit by a bat in an altercation with the House of David batboy. He was taken to Newport Hospital in a police cruiser car and three stitches were taken to the cut. He was later taken to his house." (No more is known concerning little Carl Oliver. Perhaps some "Oliver" from Newport reading this book will come forward and let us know if he was traumatized from his "religious" experience.

Major League, Bloomer Girls, Negro League and other Barnstorming Teams

As mentioned earlier, a fair amount of black baseball barnstorming teams came to Newport. This was especially so in the 1890s, when the Cuban Giants made several appearances each year. These games were always very well attended. Another barnstorming team, the Clowns, also ventured into Newport in the 1920s. Nothing more is known about this team, although I have seen it mentioned in other communities in Rhode Island. Also on the barnstorming docket were Bloomer Girl teams. Bloomer Girl baseball teams roamed the country from the 1870s through the early twentieth century, so named for the uniforms they wore. At the time, it was thought that proper women should wear skirts; however, skirts were extremely impractical to wear while playing baseball due to the potential for immodesty and because severe injury to bare legs was a real possibility. So women designed the "bloomer," which looked like a skirt but functioned like a pantaloon, maintaining both modesty and relative safety. The Bloomer Girl teams were professionals and played to make their living, usually splitting gate receipts and selling postcards like the one pictured in this book.

Almost all East Coast major-league teams brought barnstorming teams to Newport, including the Boston Red Sox, the Boston Braves, the Philadelphia Phillies, the New York Giants and, of course, the most famous barnstorming team ever, the New York Yankees team that boasted Babe Ruth and Lou

A Bloomer Girls baseball club, 1909. *Author's collection.*

Gehrig. These teams would play primarily teams from the Sunset League or semipro teams like the Trojans. Sometimes famous ballplayers would agree to come to play in a game, such as when Ty Cobb agreed to play in a game on March 23, 1920. Before Cobb would agree to play, he required a deposit to be hand-delivered to him in New York City by a Trojans team representative. The game was rained out, and, of course, the deposit was never returned. The fee for Cobb's appearance would have been $1,000, which was quite a sum for one game in 1920. Unlike Cobb, many major-league players found it necessary to supplement their income by playing on barnstorming teams or signing with semipro teams for town/city playoffs after the regular season was over.

DONKEY BASEBALL (AND A PERSONAL STORY)

(Author's note: I thank you in advance for letting me come out of my more formal prose style to share the following true story from my childhood.)

I feel the morning upon me. My gigantic hound dog, Ike, named after Dwight D. Eisenhower, is laboriously breathing, his lungs moving in and out while lying next to me. He, Ike, has taken the covers off me again. But no worries—it is a warm day. Oh, I love my dog. Suddenly, coming from the deep inner belly, I feel a tingly sensation. Why is that? Then I remember. Tonight is Donkey Baseball, the best night of the long summer. I ever so slowly and carefully open my eyes a bit. I see the rays of the sun filtering into my room with ever so tiny specks of dust floating around and reflecting the sunlight. I make the mistake of moving my hand out from underneath Ike. He rewards me with a big, slobbery kiss right on my mouth. Boy, does his breath stink—as if the bowels of the earth and all the decrepit things that live underneath have harmoniously collected in the humongous cavity

An advertisement for donkey ball at Cardines Field. *Newport Daily News*, August 21, 1939. *Author's collection.*

that is his mouth. I feel I'm going to throw up. But I don't, and I forgive. He is my dog, and I love him!

I suddenly spring up, and old Ike springs up, too, but falls directly upon me. I am six, and my dog weighs more than me. I struggle for breath and, at the same time, squeeze my dog with all the love I possibly can give with my whole body. He licks me. We tumble off the bed and onto the floor in one big jumbled mass of dog, boy, blanket and pillow. It is time to get up, and again I think of Donkey Baseball Day, the best day of the year.

I get dressed, all the time Ikie pulling at each item of clothing I try to put on. "Stop it, Ike!" I yell. Of course, that does no good. There ain't no time that dog ever lends an ear to what I have to say. Nope, no sirree! Never! If the truth be told, I am glad he doesn't listen to me. He is his own dog, and he has a right to go his own way. I always believed that.

Well, Ikie and I go about our business of the morning. We go over to say hello to my grandma and help her with the morning routine. She is old, old beyond her years. She's had a rough life. My grandma lived in a trailer behind us, partly because of her health and partly because, I believe, she is lonely. My mother, of course, was already gone to work for the day. She never had no fun as an adult, I think in my heart's mind, being, for all intents and purposes, a single parent to four kids in a small rural town in Iowa. She works long hours as a waitress. My father, when he is around, takes all her money. She is allowed to keep just enough to feed us and buy her uniforms. I feel bad for her.

I go fix breakfast for my youngest sister, and while I'm at it, I fix breakfast for my older brother (a year older) and my other younger sister (a year younger). And as for my little sister, she's what you call a handful, always causing trouble. Just the other day, she gave a closed-fist whack through the fence to the preacher's son, who is her age. He lives next door. That, and the bloody nose resulting, I can tell you did not sit well with nobody in the neighborhood. But the neighbors understood in the end, for she was kind of like my dog Ike—not of the constitution to listen to nobody.

Next, I go out to the garden and pull up those nasty, stubborn, ugly, terrible-looking weeds. Gotta be careful in the garden, for there are all kinds of snakes and big yellow-and-black spiders that live under the leaves. Yep, careful you got to be! I went and got myself bit by one of those spiders once—whooeee, not a good idea! I was downright sick for two whole days. Well, back to work. Next, I pick the ripe cucumbers. You gotta pick them before they get big an' yellow, for they are no good to nobody then. Now Ikie, he is roaming around the yard and into the cornfield behind our house lookin' for rabbits. Of course, he never caught a rabbit—the looking for them seems to entertain him enough I guess as I watch him. Sometimes I wish I were Ikie! Before I go on to the picking of the tomatoes for canning, I allow my mind drift to what was coming that night: the Donkey Baseball Game.

Now, you may be wondering why the game was so important. Before you let your mind go a-wandering, it is not because of the hilarity of watching grown-ups fall off the donkeys or the stubbornness of the donkeys refusin' to move. Nope—it's neither one of those. For in actuality, I don't see much of the game. You see, the cornfield runs perpendicular to two sides of the field—whoops, is that too big a word to use? I actually know big words. That surprises a lot of people, so I keep it a secret. I learn more that way around grownups. The reason people are surprised I have such a big vocabulary is because I can't read and won't be able to 'til I reach fifth grade. For you see, I have what would be called in the future a learning disability in the language arts. But of course teachers did not know that then—people just thought I was slow. However, for some strange reason, I always knew the meaning of very big words. Well anyway, back to our ball field story. You see, our ball field is carved out of the cornfield at the very farthest edge of town, on public property. But in small towns like this, there ain't much difference between public and private property. Actually, a ball field carved out of cornfields wasn't anything unusual in my part of the country. In fact, the whole town seemed to be carved out of a cornfield, and sometimes I would go wondering that maybe the farmers didn't want us there at all. You see, us town kids had a hard time for what were we good for. Perhaps they are right. There I go adrift in philosophy again. Later in life, I would figure out that this ill feeling wasn't coming from the farmers at all but from inner personal "issues."

Anyway, you might ask what do cornfields, baseball and donkeys have in common—oh yes, and little boys, too. Here it is. "Ikie, get out of that trash before you eat something that will turn your stomach into mush!" Sorry, got to watch that dog. People thought I was slow, but my dog—well, I don't know if there is such a thing as a slow dog, but he'd be it if there was, at least in the common-sense department. Oh yeah, you want to know about the baseballs. You see, baseballs were rare at the time. So every time a ball would go foul and head into the cornfield, our (the youngsters') job was to retrieve the ball and bring it back promptly to the white shack where the announcer, the popcorn, the candy, the pop, the scorecards and the old men baseball experts were all kept. Once the ball was deposited with the popcorn attendant, we were graciously rewarded with a nickel. On a good night, I could make a fortune—and that is why Donkey Baseball Day was so important.

Now, before you go off thinking in your head that that's an easy job, you got to learn a few facts about how it was. Most people think that a small farming town must be just about the most calmest, friendliest, delightful, beautiful place to be. Actually, it is all that. However, just like in life, it has a dark side. You might say according to our sensibilities now, it was at times a violent place. The concept of a bully is something that was equally shared among a number of young boys—probably girls, too. But I never paid much mind to that. Here's the problem and why this job of retrieving baseballs was hard and dangerous work.

As soon as the ball sailed over the shed, bleachers or backstop and into the cornfield, ten to fifteen hearty young scraps of human energy would beeline it into the cornfield. Remember, I told you I had some problems—things like reading, as well as speaking and generally a severe problem in avoiding the daydream enticement while in school. But before you go thinking I ain't no good at anything, there's one thing I was good at, and that was predicting the trajectory of a foul ball off the bat. So I was often first to find the ball nestled among the corn leaves. As a small child, I was gifted with a fair amount of speed. When I began my career of "ball retriever," I was just four years old, and I was not gifted with the understanding of stealth. So upon finding the ball, I never got back to the white shed before I was lit up by several eager and not-so-pleasant boys who would capture the ball from me. In my early years as a ball retriever, on most Donkey Baseball Days, I would come home after the game with quite large shiners on one or both eyes and perhaps a swollen cheek and a bloody lip. You probably have guessed what was the cause of my predicament. Not being of a disposition to let go, I would find myself on the wrong end of a five-fingered knuckle sandwich, which naturally resulted in the infirmities I came home with.

So, out of a sense of entrepreneurism and survival, I learnt a few things. I learned to use my skill of predicting the ball's eventual resting spot in the cornfield, I learned that I was faster than anyone else and then I learned the most valuable skill of all: stealth. I found if I could get out in the field fast enough and lay ever so close to the rich dirt of the plowed field, and thought of myself as one with the cornstalks, believe it or not, I would in essence become one with the corn. (Very Zen-like, huh?) I know in your grownup mind you may have a difficult time comprehending how this metaphysical transformation could happen in such a manner, but I swear on my poor Ikie's grave that is exactly how it happened. Therefore, because of my newfound success and the many nickels retrieved, from age five on, I always thought Donkey Baseball Day was more special than any of the day in the year—even Christmas. So, if you find yourself in a rural farming town on Donkey Baseball Day, remember the lessons that I have given to you. Oh, and here's one other important fact: ballplayers hit a ton more foul balls when they're thinking about having to get on a donkey after they hit the ball. Then they have to deal with that darn donkey, which almost certainly will either buck them off or simply not move at all.

—Ricky Harris, age six, now in a sixty-two-year-old body

Following are the rules for donkey baseball as outlined on the program for a 1940s baseball game in Baltimore between the Kiwanis Club and the traveling Donkey Baseball Club:

DONKEY BASEBALL RULES

All players except the pitcher, catcher and batter shall be mounted upon donkeys. The batter must hit the ball outside the infield to be fair, and there are no strikeouts or walks. Upon hitting a fair ball, the batter must mount a donkey to run the bases. All fielders must ride their donkeys to within one step of the ball before dismounting to retrieve it. The outfielders are permitted to throw from the ground, but infielders must remount donkeys before making a throw. All balls must be thrown to the pitcher, and he throws to other players. No balls are thrown from one player to another. The pitchers are confined to the area marked off by white lines and cannot get out of that area for any purpose. All base runners are either forced out of place or must be touched with the ball—touching the donkey of a base runner does not constitute an out. Donkeys must be ridden to the bases and not pulled by the bridle. No blocking is allowed by the basemen, and no signs or motions to frighten donkey away from bases is allowed.

I have had a fascination with donkey baseball for many years and have performed extensive research to discover its origins. Some claim that promoter Ray Doane is the inventor of the game; however, this has not been verified. A thorough digital search covering over 120 million newspaper pages has resulted in the identification of 9,850 articles in small daily and weekly newspapers from around the United States related to donkey baseball played in forty-three states, Japan and Canada. The first mention of the game comes in 1933, and no doubt its popularity was enhanced because of the comic relief it provided during the Depression era. Whether we will ever know who actually invented the game is doubtful. In 1933 alone, there were news reports of the game being played in eight states and eighteen different towns. This would indicate that either one promoter had a very busy summer or there were multiple companies in operation at the same time. In 1933, donkey baseball had single appearances in Mexico, Ohio, Missouri, Maryland, Mississippi, Minnesota and Utah. In that same year, there are references to the game being played in eleven different cities in Texas, leading one to speculate that the game likely could have originated there. Research indicates that the game was played from 1933 to 2011, the last game being played in New York.

I discovered eleven articles related to donkey baseball in Rhode Island, all from Newport between 1939 and 1973. However, this does not mean that this is the only city in which donkey baseball was played. For this time period, the digital newspaper search is limited to only the *Newport Daily News* and the *Newport Mercury*. There is no doubt that the game was played elsewhere in Rhode Island. As indicated by an August 21, 1939 advertisement from Cardines Field, the donkey baseball game was played in both in the hard-ball and softball genres. The games I witnessed in the 1950s were always played with the hard ball. One commonality was the intention to play the game in a jovial format, as demonstrated in the June 9, 1971 article that was covered in the *Newport Daily News* between the firemen and policemen of Newport.

Firemen Win with Donkeys

John Caswell, demonstrating the skill of a cowboy, coaxed "Honeypot" to circle the bases for the only run of the donkey baseball game, won by the Firemen over the Police last night at Cardines Field.

A crowd of 1,000 watched the comedy. Donkeys were determined to have their freedom, tossing their riders rodeo style en route to first base, or else moving in the wrong direction or playing dead.

Caswell's "home run" came in the first inning of the seventh frame of the Sunset Baseball League contest.

Adding to the merriment was the use of an oversize plastic bat and a wiffle ball, which confused the players with its weird flight.

Bob Westmoreland, the master of ceremonies, kept the show moving, and the game was over 10 minutes before rain fell.

Player with donkey, circa 1920. *Author's collection.*

Author's note: I chose to end this book with a bit of levity—not because I do not take baseball history seriously but because I want to avoid taking it too seriously. In so many ways, baseball is like life. It is full of facts, decisions, right and wrong turns, tragedy, comedy, joy, ecstasy, sadness and all the emotions in between. However, it is just a small part of our human experience and, in the end, simply a game—a game that we have created for pleasure and, for people like me, as an opportunity to tell stories. I hope you have enjoyed this limited expedition to a place called *Newport Baseball History: America's Pastime in the City by the Sea.*

BIBLIOGRAPHY

BOOKS

Acocella, Nicholas, and Donald Dewey. *Encyclopedia of Major League Baseball Teams*. New York: HarperCollins Publishers, 1993.

Bayles, Richard M. *History of Newport County, Rhode Island from the Year 1638 to the Year 1887*. New York: L.E. Preston Company, 1888.

Carruth, Gordon. *What Happened When: A Chronology of Life and Events in America*. New York: Signet, 1991.

Chadwick, Henry. *Beadle's Dime Base-Ball Player*. New York: Beadle & Company Publishers, 1867.

Channing, George G. *Early Recollections of Newport, R.I. from the Year 1793 to 1811*. Newport, RI: A.J. Ward and Charles E. Hammet Jr., 1868.

Charlton, James. *The Baseball Chronology*. New York: Macmillan Publishing Company, 1991.

Conley, Patrick T. *An Album of Rhode Island History, 1636–1986*. Virginia Beach, VA: Donning Company Publishers, 1992.

Dickson, Paul. *The Dickson Baseball Dictionary*. New York: Facts on File, 1989.

Dix, John Ross. *A Handbook of Newport and Rhode Island*. Newport, RI: C.E. Hammett Jr., 1852.

Federal Writers' Project (WPA). *Rhode Island: A Guide to the Smallest State*. Boston: Houghton Mifflin Company, 1937.

Gershman, Michael Diamonds. *The Evolution of the Ballpark*. Boston: Houghton Mifflin Company, 1993.

Gettelson, Leonard. *One for the Book: All-Time Baseball Records*. N.p.: The Sporting News, 1954.

Goodwin, Doris Kearns. *The Bully Pulpit: Theodore Roosevelt, William Howard Taft, and the Golden Age of Journalism*. New York: Simon & Schuster, 2013.

Haley, John Williams. *"The Old Stone Bank" History of Rhode Island*. 4 vols. Providence, RI: Providence Institution for Savings, 1929–44.

Harris, Frank, G. *History of the Re-Union of the Sons and Daughters of the Revolution*. Newport, RI: Davis & Pitman, 1885.

Harris, Rick. *Brown University Baseball: A Legacy of the Game*. Charleston, SC: The History Press, 2012.

———. *Rhode Island Baseball: The Early Years*. Charleston, SC: The History Press, 2008.

Herrick, Wier, and Harvey White. *Fun & Games of Long Ago*. Reprint. Maynard, MA: Chandler Press, 1988.

Johnson, Lloyd. *Baseball's Book of Firsts*. Philadelphia: Courage Books, 1999.

Johnson, Lloyd, and Miles Wolff. *The Encyclopedia of Minor League Baseball*. Durham, NC: Baseball America Inc., 1997.

Kellner, George H., and Stanley J. Lemons. *Rhode Island, the Ocean State: An Illustrated History*. Sun Valley, CA: American Historical Press, 2004.

Laswell, George D. *Corners and Characters of Rhode Island.* Providence, RI: Oxford Press, 1924.

Lawton, Herbert A. *Historic Newport.* Newport, RI: Newport Chamber of Commerce, 1933.

Levin, Leonard. *Days of Greatness: Providence Baseball, 1875–1885.* Cooperstown, NY: Society for American Baseball Research, 1984.

Lewine, Harris, and Daniel Okrent. *The Ultimate Baseball Book.* Boston: Houghton Mifflin Company, 1979.

Lewis, Rob. *Images of America: Newport.* Charleston, SC: Arcadia Publishing, 1996.

Macmillan Publishing Company. *The Baseball Encyclopedia.* New York: Macmillan Publishing Company, 1990.

Madden, W.C. *The Women of the All-American Girls Professional Baseball League.* Jefferson, NC: McFarland & Company Inc., 1997.

Mason, George. *Newport Illustrated.* Newport, RI: C.A. Alvord, printer, 1884.

McKissack, Patricia C., and Frederick McKissack Jr. *Black Diamond: The Story of the Negro Baseball Leagues.* New York: Scholastic Inc., 1998.

Mercurio, John A. *Record Profiles of Baseball Hall of Famers.* New York: Harper & Row, 1990.

Nemec, David. *Great Baseball Feats, Facts & Firsts.* New York: Signet Classics, 1989.

Okkonen, Marc. *The Federal League of 1914–1915: Baseball's Third Major League.* Cooperstown, NY: Society for American Baseball Research, 1989.

O'Neal, Bill. *The International League: A Baseball History, 1884–1991.* Austin, TX: Eakin Press, 1992.

Pietrusza, David, Matthew Silverman and Michael Gershman. *Baseball: The Biographical Encyclopedia.* New York: Total/Sports Illustrated, 2000.

BIBLIOGRAPHY

Rebok, Barbara, and Doug Rebok. *Early Days in Newport, Rhode Island.* N.p.: A Plus Printing Company, n.d.

Rhode Island Historical Preservation Commission. "The Southern Thames Street Neighborhood in Newport, Rhode Island." Statewide Historical Preservation Report N-N-3, February 1880.

Solomon, Burt. *The Baseball Timeline.* New York: DK, 2001.

Soos, Troy. *Before the Curse: The Glory Days of New England Baseball, 1858–1918.* Hyannis, MA: Parnassus Imprints, 1997.

Stanford, Les. *Desperate Sons.* New York: HarperCollins Publishers, 2012.

State of Rhode Island. *Know Rhode Island: Facts Concerning the Land of Roger Williams.* Providence, RI: Oxford Press, 1931.

Sullivan, Dean A. *Early Innings: A Documentary History of Baseball, 1825–1908.* Lincoln, NE: Bison Books, 1997.

Voigt, David Q. *Baseball: An Illustrated History.* University Park: Pennsylvania State University Press, 1987.

Warburton, Eileen. *In Living Memory: A Chronicle of Newport, Rhode Island, 1888–1988.* Newport, RI: Newport Savings and Loan Association/Island Trust Company, 1988.

Wright, Marshall D. *The International League, 1884–1953.* Jefferson, NC: McFarland & Co., 1998.

MAPS

Atlas & Surveys of the State of Rhode Island & Providence Plantations. Philadelphia: Everts & Richards, 1895.

Atlas of the State of Rhode Island & Providence Plantations. Philadelphia: D.G. Beers & Co., 1870.

New York, 1880–1951. New York: Sanborn Map Co., 1951.

Bibliography

Newspapers, Periodicals and Journals

Harper's Weekly (1857–1920
Newport Daily News (1873–2013)
Newport Journal and Weekly News (1917–18)
Newport Mercury (1885–1974)
Newport Mercury and Weekly News (1928–1977)
Newport Naval Log (1974–1977)
Providence Evening Press (1872–1877)
Providence Journal (Bulletin) (1860–1996)
Woonsocket (Evening) Call (1894–1927)
Woonsocket Evening Reporter (1908)

Websites

www.ancestry.com
www.baseball-reference.com
www.charliesballparks.com/stadiums.htm
www.gdsunsetleague.pointstreaksites.com/view/gdsunsetleague
www.la84.org/sports-library-digital-collection
http://library.salve.edu/archives/archives_collections.html
www.loc.gov/pictures
www.newspaperarchive.com
www.pointstreaksites.com/view/newportgulls/cardines-field/baseball-in-
    newport
www.salveathletics.com/sports/bsb/archive

Yearbooks

The Lance (St. Georges School), 1899–2013
Regina Maris (Salve Regina University), 1981–2013

INDEX

INDEX

INDEX

INDEX

INDEX

World War II 53, 104, 132, 135
Wrigley Field 104

Y

YMCA 102

About the Author

Richard "Rick" Nyle Harris was born and raised in Iowa. He obtained a BA degree in painting and drawing and, later, a master's in social work. He has been an adjunct professor at the Rhode Island College School of Social Work since 1993. He is also an adjunct professor at Salve Regina University, where he teaches several courses, including two baseball courses looking at the sociological, historical and cultural aspects of baseball in America. In addition to teaching part time, Rick works full time as the executive director of the Rhode Island chapter of the National Association of Social Workers.

Rick began his baseball research and writing career in 1992. He has authored *Rhode Island Baseball: The Early Years* (The History Press, 2008), *Brown University Baseball: A Legacy of the Game* (The History Press, 2012) and four other self-published books on baseball. He has presented at numerous baseball research conferences, provided countless public talks, written many articles and made several appearances on local television news shows. He is also credited with an appearance as a historic baseball expert in the documentary film by David Bettencourt titled *You Must Be This Tall: The Story of Rocky Point Park*. Rick is a member of the Society for American Baseball Research (SABR) and the Rhode Island Historical Society.

Rick lives in Cranston, Rhode Island. He met his marriage partner, Peg, a Rhode Island native, in 1974 and moved to Rhode Island that same year. Peg and Rick have two wonderful children, Emily and Jacob, and a very sweet dog named Fluffy.